WHAT DID YOU THINK WAS GOING TO HAPPEN?

The Betrayal of South Central

Uncovering four decades of
corruption by government and political
and judicial officials - and finally exposing their
systemic racism in the city's failure
to allow cable TV in LA's
poorest neighborhood

Clinton E. Galloway

ISBN (paperback) 978-1-7357076-0-0
ISBN (ebook) 978-1-7357076-1-7
ISBN (audiobook) 978-1-7357076-2-4

Published by Phoenix Publishing Corp.

To Donna:
thanks for your support
in battle and story

CONTENTS

PREFACE

At the age of six, in my mother's kitchen, I screamed because I burned my finger putting it in the flame on the stove. My brother had told me if I put my finger in the yellow part of the flame, and not the blue, I wouldn't be burned. My mother was unimpressed with my reasoning. As she got the first-aid cream to soothe my aching finger, she looked at me with a sense of wonderment and asked, "What did you think was going to happen?"

Abundantly obvious answers seem only to confuse us of late, as we look for answers to great social questions we face as a nation. But by ignoring the obvious, we are in fact ignoring the simplicity of the problem, only to, inevitably, complicate the answers. Turning a simple explanation for a simple problem into a complex issue is the way the government disguises its lack of desire or ability to solve problems. This is especially true in the Black community.

People try to say you don't see something that is in front of your face. But I disagree. It's a lie, and what they're telling you is a lie. The obvious is the obvious for a reason. Politicians, especially since the 1950s and 1960s, have pretended the obvious answers to problems don't exist. In fact, it's good judgment that doesn't exist in their system of thinking. An examination of their

7

politically driven behavior during this period of time will clearly indicate today's social results, which were put in motion many years ago.

This book's primary focus is Black America, media, the First Amendment to the Bill of Rights, and the betrayal of Los Angeles South Central community. Since honoring civil rights is a matter of law, the question becomes why governments sought to deprive the poorest citizens within the city of Los Angeles their constitutional rights. South Central Los Angeles is an example of what happens to a community when corrupt politicians deprive citizens of the civil rights guaranteed by the Constitution of the United States. For example, my case to provide cable service to the South Central community could not have been denied without the complicity of City of Los Angeles and county officials and a federal judge of limited integrity. The proof of this matter is contained in the court records.

The First Amendment to the Constitution is not being adjudicated here. But the First Amendment guarantees the right to free speech and a free press suited to the community that it serves. Free speech and a free press allow a citizen to petition a government to identify, change, and correct its behavior, instead of allowing for the mistreatment of the citizens due to unjust control that a lack of representation allows. This is the right to seek redress.

Chapter 1

BEGINNING THE TECH REVOLUTION

I am a Black man and I am writing this book because something is seriously wrong with the Black community throughout the United States—and I think I know part of the reasons why. The same problems in Black America that existed forty years ago are much worse today and still have no resolution. We need to look at the whys.

I believe my case, which started forty years ago, is a blueprint to understand those problems—and what went wrong. A small group of citizens based out of South Central Los Angeles, of which I was one, saw an opportunity to dramatically change some of the problems in our own community by bringing technology to South Central Los Angeles. It's a tragedy of lost opportunities, affecting almost two generations of citizens there.

In 1980, we, as a group of mostly minority business people, first approached the City of Los Angeles to take advantage of the new technology at the time and develop a cable television system for the South Central area. We wanted to address current community issues: poverty, lack of education, poor health, and high crime. Unfortunately, in our case, the City of Los Angeles deprived the poorest community in Los Angeles of their basic civil rights provided to them under the Constitution of the United States and perpetuated these troubling issues. Remember, politicians and community activists are continually calling for others to give them their constitutional rights.

Now, at a time when people are making charges against others for events that were birthed thirty to forty years ago, I now feel justified in bringing up the issues that occurred in South Central Los Angeles. These issues led to the detriment and destruction of South Central Los Angeles, which might also be considered as affecting the welfare of numerous other minority communities in the United States. South Central is only a glaring, bold, and clear example of the treatment of minority communities throughout the United States.

I am not just making allegations about the loss of my civil rights, and the rights of my business partners, but also the rights of all the citizens of South Central. This is a matter of fact contained in the court records of the US District Court (Case #83-5846), the Ninth Circuit Court of Appeals (case number (Case #754 f 2d 1396 9th Circuit 1985), and the United States Supreme Court (Case #476 US 488) in the case of *City of Los Angeles v. Preferred Communications*. The fact is the government was able to violate the civil rights of half a million people for ten years and obstruct a 9–0 decision of the Supreme Court of the United States. After ten years of being segregated and having the rights of half a million people ignored, we were found to have won the case and proved that our constitutional rights had been violated. As a penalty for depriving us of our rights, we were awarded damages by the court. Federal Judge Consuelo

Marshall awarded us one dollar, one thin dollar, for a decade of our commitment and battle. The insult and loss of rights proffered by Judge Marshall illustrates the mistreatment of the South Central community, which in many cases had no rights. If your rights have no value, then you have no rights.

These records are kept in the US District Court for the Central District of California based in Los Angeles, the Ninth Circuit Court of Appeals, and the United States Supreme Court. All of these entities have issued opinions relative to this case. As usual, Black America knows nothing about it because they have been denied their right to First Amendment freedom of the press. Did you ever hear about it?

So many years have passed since South Central lost its chance for cable television technology. That was forty years ago, and, unfortunately, nothing has changed since except the name of the community from South Central Los Angeles to South Los Angeles.

As a Black man in America, I have witnessed indignities and injustices. Because I am a Black man in America, I feel both justified and obligated to make this information known to all of America. This is not an allegation but a matter of law. The law is based upon three years of involvement with the City of Los Angeles, in addition to ten years in federal court trying to achieve the utilization of our constitutional rights and get a cable operating license from the City of Los Angeles. The effect of a decade of deprivation of civil rights and technology on the South Central community would be disastrous.

The Supreme Court issued a ruling for *City of Los Angeles v. Preferred Communications* in 1986 that stated, "The limiting of access to public right-of-ways for the dissemination of information to only one person or group when there is room for more than one is a violation of the Constitution of the United States." In 1992, six years after the Supreme Court's ruling, US District Court Judge Consuelo Marshall, who was appointed by Democratic President Jimmy Carter, finally agreed that the City of Los Angeles had violated the rights we sought for more than ten years.

This is a textbook case of the process of institutionalized and systemic racism. The institutionalized racism came about when the City of Los Angeles (the institution) segregated an entire race of people. After segregating Black citizens, the City of Los Angeles would deny this community their First Amendment rights and access to the new technology being provided to the rest of the citizens within Los Angeles. The denial of rights was led by Black officials, elected and otherwise, of the City of Los Angeles, thereby using the power and resources of the City of Los Angeles to the detriment of the South Central community.

The "systemic" portion of the racism occurred as the citizens of South Central sought protection from the federal court system against the actions of the City of Los Angeles. The federal court system (systemic) was the venue for seeking protection from the racist actions of the City of Los Angeles in denying South Central electronic information via cable that was available to all other communities in Los Angeles. Our case dragged through the courts, including the US Supreme Court, for ten years. At no time were we allowed a trial by jury, our Seventh Amendment right, because the judge refused. The merits of the case were heard by two federal appellate court panels, no regular citizens. Of the twelve appellate justices who heard the merits of the case, all twelve ruled against the City of

Los Angeles. After the unanimous victory in the US Supreme Court, the case was referred back to the US District Court in Los Angeles, but I feel the judge used every delaying technique conceived of to prevent the true facts of the case from being known to the public.

The only judge to side with the racist city in its treatment of South Central Los Angeles was a Black federal judge by the name of Consuelo Marshall. As a Black jurist, she, as all federal judges are, is a representative and agent of the US court system and is supposed to provide, by oath, protection to those whose rights have been abused, stolen, or ignored. Since her power is based upon the US federal court system, her rulings should properly represent that system. I believe hers did not. The racist behavior she showed in our case was again systemic because it represented the larger court system.

In seeking relief from these unfair court proceedings, we also sought relief from law enforcement authorities, including the Los Angeles Police Department (LAPD) and the FBI. The worst treatment handed down in this entire thirteen-year process came from Black elected officials and a Black federal judge. The racism is still institutional and systemic, but it is Black-on-Black racism.

In late 1980, we were making the rounds at City Hall to get a chance to meet each of the fifteen city council members that would be deciding our license. At that time we met with Peggy Stevenson, who was a member of the Los Angeles City Council, to explain our involvement with cable television. She asked about our acceptance by other city council members who were Black and whose districts were covered in South Central. We explained behavior that we had encountered from elected officials and their deputies relative to the ownership of our cable television company. Upon hearing about the behavior of the offices of certain Black city council members she informed us that she believed the behavior was criminal and that she was obligated by law to inform the LAPD.

Less than a week later we were contacted by Detective Sergeants Domino and Ramirez from the bunco forgery division of the LAPD. They explained that it was their responsibility to look into cases of potential political crimes. After a one-hour discussion with them, we were told that there was sufficient evidence to forward the case on to the Los Angeles district attorney for potential prosecution.

The corruption that was so prevalent in Los Angeles City Hall was known to the district attorney, Gil Garcetti. Because the matter had been referred to Gil Garcetti by the LAPD, he was forced to conduct an investigation of the charges. Garcetti said that he could not proceed because the accused refused to cooperate. When stopping political corruption is not in the public interest, the corruption will continue. It has continued for forty years with no end in sight. The only limitation to the corruption in City Hall has been the federal government and the FBI. The Los Angeles district attorney has turned a blind eye to political corruption for at least the last forty years, regardless of the occupant of that office.

In late 1980, we had still not heard anything from the Los Angeles district attorney or from the California attorney general. We contacted both parties regarding cable television and potential violations of the law being perpetrated by elected officials. At that time we decided to contact the FBI because the behavior represented a constitutional violation as well as potential issues of criminal violation. When we met with the FBI they were already familiar with some of what was going on downtown. We were additionally given warnings by the FBI regarding potential conflicts with some of the players on the opposite side of this matter. One of the warnings was that we should not live within the city of Los Angeles because Tom Bradley had many friends in the LAPD.

The story of how the rights were lost is contained in my book *Anatomy of a Hustle: Cable Comes to South Central L.A.*, which was published in 2012. Many of the leading Black politicians, not only in California but throughout the United States, made sure the deprivation of the constitutional rights of South Central citizens was completed. Politicians, even though they do not represent California, are certainly aware of civil rights cases affecting Black Americans that are heard by the US Supreme Court. The book explains how this was able to happen in a free society without any interest by civil rights organizations or by Black leadership in general.

No one knew about this case or seemed to care. Not the Black leadership of this nation, not the political party that says it cares about Black America, and not the American media, which we were trying to gain participation in for the benefit of the people of South Central Los Angeles. A few years after the Supreme Court case was decided, the *Wall Street Journal* published a major article about the case. In 1992, *Reader's Digest*, the largest general publication magazine in the United States, published a three-page article about the case and potential effects on people within the poorest part of Los Angeles. Black media consisting of newspapers and magazines completely ignored the case.

The entrenched media, then and now, determines what is seen

by America. Unfortunately, minorities have only a very limited ownership interest in all media platforms and networks, and these are not equally distributed based upon the population in the United States. In other words, although Black America represents 10–12 percent of the population, it certainly does not control 10–12 percent of the media that is presented to it.

The Democratic Party, in its various historical names and forms, is one of the two parties that have controlled America since its inception. The party is often described as liberal, progressive, and civil rights-oriented. This is the image they would like you to have of their principles and core beliefs. My criticism is that the Democratic Party, since the right to vote was granted to all Black citizens, has been in almost total control of Black American governance.

The Democratic Party has become little more than a political powerhouse, with its money, power, and entrenched leadership, including entrenched Black leadership, willing to turn a blind eye to the corruption that exists within its own ranks. For six years, from 1986 to 1992, the Democratic Party was remarkably silent about the technology deficit and abuses being dealt to Black citizens in South Central - unlike their non-Black neighborhoods. There was little local publicity, except by major national publications, regarding the Preferred Communications case and our efforts to help the South Central community.

I criticize the Democratic Party because it was the party in power and controlling the activities that went on during the deprivation of the rights of the citizens of South Central Los Angeles, as it still does today. I contend members of the community were denied their rights, which were given to Democratic Party insiders who were able to sell those rights to their friends and thereby limit access to the media by the community itself.

16

This book is another clarion call to Black people, from the echoes of the earlier civil rights movement, to those who are seeking their rights. We as a class of people have been mistreated and had our rights taken away—in the light of day. We should not tolerate the ongoing mistreatment of an entire race of people to serve politicians and their political party.

Where was the call for diversity when the control of distribution was being decided? Where were the civil rights groups that are so prominent in the call for diversity now, such as the NAACP and the Urban League? They were aware of the situation and they chose to support the elected officials who were taking the rights of the citizens of South Central Los Angeles, to the detriment of the community.

Black America must examine new delivery systems available through streaming the internet. There must be a substantial capital investment in order to make the situation prosper. It is not a mom-and-pop operation but rather a sophisticated business enterprise that deals with programming as well as delivery systems. It is important we control the media that is delivering the message to our young men and women. Without some degree of control over the media that influences our children and young people, we have limited influence in their lives, but we bear the responsibility for their behavior.

My partners and I not only lost our rights in an effort to serve the South Central community, but the rights of half a million people in South Central Los Angeles were also lost. Half a million people! Taking the civil rights of a single person diminishes the rights of the entire group the person represents. The people of South Central needed this cable technology in order to improve their condition and to give them opportunities to improve the community in this technological age. The technology would have given them a part of the economic system operating beyond their community and throughout the United States. The denial of access to the economic order and modern technology, along with the creation of illegal economics of drugs, gangs, and incarcerations, has led to the mass genocide and criminal behavior prevalent in low-income urban minority communities. The effect of cutting off legal means by intimidation, poor education, and the burden of prison records serves to deny South Central residents access to mainstream jobs, education, and upward mobility. The conversations of all politicians over the last forty years have not changed the basic economic principle that people need certain things to live.

More than forty years ago, in response to this very same call for diversity, my business partners and I put together a group of Black professionals and entertainment people to take advantage of the new technology. The new technology, cable television, would allow local communities to bypass the broadcast system and provide programming on a more direct and informative basis for their community. The battle to provide this delivery service was fought against by the City of Los Angeles, Black politicians, and the Democratic Party. These groups were sure that Black America would not be able to speak for itself in regard to its own development and issues that were relevant to that community.

Tens of millions of dollars and thirteen years later it became clear that there would be no involvement of Black America in the cable television industry in the city of Los Angeles. The very same people who are now calling for diversity are the ones who prevented the true ability to have diversity, which

18

was ownership. The call for diversity cannot truly be answered when there is no structural change in media control.

The growth of any new technological industry presents numerous paths to individual economic and social improvement, but you cannot take any of the paths if you are prohibited from participating in the technology cycle. Cable television was potentially revolutionary and opportunity-laden in South Central, and the equivalent of modern internet, but the South Central community had only over-the-air television. Cable television was an opportunity to expand knowledge and communication within the community in order to better allow the community to get to know itself. I felt that as communities began to understand the issues in their community, through the opportunities of two public access channels allowed to each cable licensee, they would be able to solve issues on a local basis as opposed to requiring a citywide effort, which would never come to local minority communities.

Many Black people no longer feel they are part of a nation but rather feel isolated and deserted because political promises are infrequently kept and they're treated in a different fashion than the rest of society. When any group of people does not have the same rights as the majority of citizens within a nation, you have a group that is disenfranchised. When the government has taken all steps to assure a group or community cannot obtain the rights necessary to operate in a free society, we are operating under a tyranny.

Whether the treatment is at the hands of Whites or Blacks doesn't really matter. In South Central, it was at the hands of Black politicians and appointed judges. The end result is that people who feel the failure of government are the ones who suffer. They lose their ability to educate the children and their ability to establish moral values within their own community. I certainly do not want the children of South Central to develop values established by local government officials and most elected Black politicians.

This book concerns the history and the effects of the deprivation of technology rights of the citizens of South Central. This book clearly shows the results of that deprivation of constitutional rights. This is just one issue, in one part of one city, and in one industry. There are many issues and many industries in this morass. The commonality of these issues is that Black people have been denied the right to enter the economic marketplace of America and our cable fight illustrates just how it is done.

The denial of technology to the most underprivileged group within a society is abhorrent and is carried out only by those who have morals lower than that of a rabid jackal. I ask the jackal to please excuse my denigrating language.

If I were not a Black man writing this information, I would be labeled by the media, the Democratic Party, and Black politicians as a racist. I would of course say that it is the media, the Democratic Party, and Black politicians who are in fact the racists, in this and in many other situations, because they single out Black Americans to be treated in a different fashion than the rest of America.

Chapter 2

THE BETRAYERS: BLACK LEADERSHIP AND THE DEMOCRATIC PARTY

First we must define what leadership is, and then, who is a leader. Leadership is the action of leading a group or an organization. The first purpose of leadership is to guide a group of people toward a common goal. We often speak of leaders, but what does it really mean when a person is supposed to be our leader? Many people have spoken of leadership. We hear it in sports, politics, business, and anywhere there is a group working for a common goal. A second purpose of leadership is to maximize the efforts of a group.

Former New York Knick and US Senator Bill Bradley said on the subject, "Leadership is unlocking people's potential to become better." Martin Luther King Jr. said, "A genuine leader is not a searcher for consensus but a molder of consensus." These two quotes give a good idea of what leadership should be. Unfortunately the supposed leadership within the Black community has no concept of what leadership entails.

When I think of the current Black leadership, the terms *integrity* and *honesty* do not come to my mind. The terms *selfish* and *egomaniacal* do. Leadership that doesn't work concretely for a goal is not in fact leadership, but exploitation. They prey on those who are not able to protect themselves and promise great things. But the spigot doesn't flow, it only drips … and the drips are for the ones who favor the leadership.

While none of us like robbers, we have a special dislike for those robbers who steal from the poor or the elderly. That is where we are with Black leadership in America today. They are willing to sacrifice the futures, and have already sacrificed many futures over the last forty years, of young Black citizens in order to seek higher office and get more campaign contributions to utilize for their own selfish purposes. The same people are in power now in South Central as were during the 1980s and 1990s.

In terms of leadership, I will limit my explanations about leadership to the Los Angeles area and California in general. It is clear when the number two city in the United States has a corruption problem that many cities might have or develop if they follow LA.

In recent months, several FBI raids at Los Angeles City Hall sought city paperwork regarding behavior related to questionable uses of City Hall power. There have been investigations of individual council members and investigations of the city itself for its behavior. One city councilman has already pleaded guilty to corruption charges in 2020. The former chief deputy of another city councilman has also pleaded guilty to corruption charges. It is anticipated that a second city councilman will be indicted within the next few months. The offices of two of the fifteen Los Angeles City Council members have had persons plead guilty for their criminal behavior in Los Angeles City Hall. The FBI has also raided the homes of city council members in search of evidence regarding their behavior as part of the Los Angeles City Council.

The Los Angeles Times said most recently, on May 28, 2020, that the Los Angeles City Council is in danger of being viewed as a "pay-to-play" government that is perceived by the public to be corrupt. The same behavior has been going on for forty years at least, but now everyone wants to act surprised. There is no surprise to this: a corrupt organization does corrupt things.

Watch your close friends, and your enemies can't do you any harm. This is an old line from music as well as literature, and it proves true even today. Your leaders can lead you to hell and tell you they've got you in heaven if you don't know any better and don't watch what they are doing.

My comments describe an entire political party, the Democratic Party, and are not directed against any particular individual other than those I have specifically mentioned. The system has allowed this sort of behavior to go on over a forty-year period. You will notice it is federal authorities finding the criminals in Los Angeles City Hall—not the local officials. The district attorney's office and the state attorney general don't appear to be capable of stopping this criminal behavior, which has run rampant. Without any notice or concern by the media, these marks of shame on justice may soon affect or have already affected many more Americans than just Black America.

The majority of politicians who claim to be representing minority areas are members of the Democratic Party. In the forty years I have dealt with and watched Los Angeles politics, it is clear the elected officials have gone astray. These politicians offer little more than fronts for the ongoing mistreatment of these same minorities they claim to represent. The supposition of Black leadership is merely that: a supposition. There is little evidence that exists to support it. Their leadership has not led to many benefits in the Black community over the last forty years. In fact, things have gotten worse as more Black leaders have taken office. Part of the problem is these Black leaders remain in office for decades and do nothing but get rich. When they leave office, they often pass their seat or office to their children or other relatives, as if they were royalty of some sort.

The support of Blacks for the Democratic Party is overwhelming, and any action to take that control will be dealt with drastically. This includes taking the rights of anyone who would seek to exercise their constitutional rights to expose a corrupt political party. I say corrupt, and make no mistake about it, the Democratic Party, to me, resembles any other criminal organization. They lie, bend, and break the law continuously. Simply look at the indictment of elected officials at the California state level over the last five years and you will see a percentage substantially higher than criminal indictments of the general population.

Black politicians think Black Americans are merely lemmings to be led over the cliff for their economic benefit. The Democratic Party is fully aware of this behavior but is afraid to bring up anything regarding Black leaders for fear of being called racist. In my opinion, Black leadership ignored the rights of the citizens of South Central who needed technology at the same time as non-minority neighborhoods. Black politicians are the ones who have been making sure we cannot benefit from our constitutional rights.

The Democratic Party cannot take chances with the Black vote because it is a sizable portion of their voting base. They use their front men, aka minority politicians, to enforce their will within the community. They get votes for the Democratic Party regardless of whether they benefit the constituents and voters or not. The same approach is applicable at the local, state, and national levels of government. You need only look at the percentage of Blacks who vote for the Democratic Party to understand why they need to maintain this voting bloc in order to maintain any control of power. A disclosure of the behavior by the Democratic Party and its major leaders such as the late Tom Bradley would serve to undermine the confidence that Black America has always placed with the Democratic Party. In my opinion this confidence is misplaced to a great extent.

The Democratic Party seemed to recognize the risk of Black America having the ability to communicate for itself. Is that the reason they denied access to the technology necessary for the growth of any community for twenty years? There was a great risk to Democratic Party power if the politicians under their control were exposed. The Black vote was critical for all plans of the Democratic Party, and remains so today. And so, in order to protect their control of the Black vote, they were willing to deprive Black citizens of their civil and constitutional rights. Instead of the community being able to control its own communication media and flow of information, these tools would be controlled by the friends and large contributors of elected officials.

As mentioned earlier, Democratically controlled cities like New York and Los Angeles made sure prominent, supportive members and donors of their own political party were given a monopoly over the new technology, cable television. This was especially true in areas that were predominantly Black or dominated by minorities. Access to a free press, cable television, and other electronic media may give the community access to information that would help them better judge elected officials who were supposed to be providing leadership.

Most Black communities in the United States are controlled by the Democratic Party politically. This control runs from local elections to national elections to the control of city, county, state, and federal government agencies. With such power and control comes a level of responsibility to the citizens who have voted for you to obtain this power. The failure to responsibly utilize this power is a tragedy, and that tragedy shows itself every day in urban and minority communities.

The Democratic Party, based upon their rhetoric, is supposed to be representing Black America, and therefore my criticism is of those who claim to be representing Black America as opposed to those who never claimed they were representing Black America. Black America has never claimed or believed it was going to get support from the Republican Party. This is partially because of the Democratic Party's push to have everyone in the Republican Party identified as racist or against the average citizen. What is more racist than the denial of technology to those who need it most ... and when will the Black community realize this?

Black Democrats stay in public office at the federal level essentially for life. There are term limits at the state and local levels. Look and see how the politicians merely rotate elected positions between city, county, and state in order to stay in office somewhere. Therefore, all the people who remain in power in places like the Congressional Black Caucus are the same ones who ignored Supreme Court rulings that had a dramatic effect upon South Central and all Black Americans living there.

The Democratic Party has controlled Black citizens' access to the political system since the 1930s. While Democratic efforts were appreciated during the 1960s, Black America must consider the need for new help in this rapidly changing world. In the 1960s, the Democratic Party supported the War on Poverty. How has that worked out? What have they done for the community lately? Opportunities to improve communities are denied by behind-the-scenes events that no one will bring to the light of day.

In California, the Democratic Party decided it was in their best interests to silence any voice of potential dissent from within Black America. How is it that media in minority communities is never owned by the minorities? The first justification given is that it costs too much money for them to own media. That is grossly untrue because there are many wealthy Black people in the United States who can provide capital to enterprises that will benefit their communities. The City of Los Angeles also acknowledged in writing, as early as 1980, that at least one minority company had sufficient capital to construct a cable television system in South Central: Preferred Communications, my partnership. But we didn't get the license. Why?

In 1994, the Democratic Party and President Bill Clinton created a national crime bill that brought dramatic and long-lasting negative effects upon Black communities throughout the United States. The draconian measures that were used by the government in order to incarcerate young Black men were a disgrace but were done under the pretext of the war on drugs. This was another extension of the war on drugs and minorities.

The Democratic Party wanted to appear to be hard on crime to the general populace and made laws that would decimate entire communities by locking up young men for unbelievable amounts of time—in stark contrast to reasonable sentencing guidelines. When it comes to Black people, government always wants to take a hard stand to make an example, but they do not make an example when it comes to educational opportunity. This new crime bill was merely an extension of the drug war that had been declared by President Richard Nixon.

The bill, titled the Violent Crime Control and Law Enforcement Act, would lead to the wholesale incarceration of young Black men and other minorities. Many of the people they sought to incarcerate were the "lowest rung on this war," merely the foot soldiers who had no idea who the real drug powerbrokers were. The lower levels of gangs had been created with the assistance of the policies of the government itself. This legislation would serve to increase the prison population by more than 20 percent over a ten-year period because of the extended sentences that were meted out to those of color and without money.

The new crime bill had a disproportionate impact upon minority communities, increasing the sentences for Black people by creating a different level of criminal offense for powdered cocaine and crack cocaine. Crack cocaine, which was used and predominantly sold in poor and minority areas, would lead to sentences five times as long as for those who faced powdered cocaine charges. There was a difference between these two types of cocaine: one was used primarily by those with money, and the other was used primarily by those without money. It is not hard to calculate where the Black population would fall in this equation. The cheaper one, crack, merely involves adding baking soda and therefore has less cocaine per pound than pure cocaine.

Cocaine is the substance that is illegal—not the use of baking soda. The harsher treatment of drug addicts and small-time drug dealers shows the severe penalties imposed upon the poor and minority persons who became involved in the criminal justice system. It demonstrated a new way for the federal government to incarcerate young Black men for longer periods of time.

Once again, the Black citizens of the United States were not able to publicize their feelings about the effects of this crime bill upon themselves, their families, and the community. The lack of First Amendment rights limited their knowledge of what was going on with their representatives.

The bill also created increased penalties for those that were deemed to be gang members. The designation of gang enhancement was such a broad and general term that its enforcement was subject to a local police force only. This was an easy tag because anybody who knows someone Black can be called a gang member in Black America. In my opinion, the gang enhancement penalties were used to extend incarceration, mainly for minorities, as another excuse to support the increased use of private prisons.

This legislation also created special designations for "gang-related activity" for those who were deemed to be part of a gang—the definition of which was unclear. There was no need to prove a person was part of a gang; law enforcement simply had to state that a person was part of a gang. This would enhance sentencing for whatever crime was alleged to have been committed—adding five to ten years to the prison sentence of predominantly minority offenders. The numbers will show the gang enhancement penalties were used primarily against minorities and specifically against Black people. This

29

was also the plan of the Democratic Party—to show the party was tough on crime, especially when it involved Black people.

Crack, because of its addictive nature, became an epidemic in urban and minority communities, spurred on by its low cost. Addiction is now classified as a crime instead of an illness. This crack epidemic assisted with the development of gangs within the community because of the money made by gangs in low-income neighborhoods through the sale of illegal drugs. The illegal nature of the drug and the disparate treatment received by sellers of the drug encouraged them to join organizations to protect their business in the process. The epidemic became a series of gangs that were militarized. The militarized police force would battle gangs with the community caught in the middle. Those addicted to drugs were forgotten during the war on drugs. What should be a medical issue was instead a battle for survival from drugs and guns. The gangs protected themselves with more sophisticated weapons, and the police became more militarized to protect themselves and fight the gangs.

In 1996, the federal government passed another law. People who had been convicted of felonies with drugs could no longer apply for food stamp assistance or any other government benefit once they got out of prison. In my opinion, the federal government would do everything they could to force ex-convicts back into criminal activities in order to simply feed themselves. This policy would serve to increase recidivism and an early return to prison. This policy did not apply to mass murderers or child rapists but only to those who had been involved with drugs.

The drug business is a widely used term that encompasses everything from heroin to marijuana to pills. The policy of grouping all drugs into one category is the equivalent of saying shoplifting is the same as armed robbery. This seems to be applicable only to people with drug issues, who are predominantly minorities in most jurisdictions. Many of these people were caught up in the system because of their own drug habit and inability to cope with their addiction. Drug crimes were prosecuted more vigorously and prosecutors sought longer sentences against minorities. The sentencing was more severe for Blacks, despite the fact that the use of drugs was basically the same percentage among all segments of society.

Who is going to use more drugs than a person who is miserable, poor, and living in a war zone? Living with stress and in a war zone could naturally cause mental illness and substance abuse, making the minority citizens as afraid of the police as they were of gangs. The citizens were caught between warring factions. One wanted to sell them drugs and the other wanted to imprison them for taking drugs.

Look carefully at the politicians who represent you. Are they representing the average citizen of any race, or not? Are they representing those who give them large contributions in order to buy their time and attention? The Los Angeles County Democratic Party is a classic example of the latter behavior. Money talks.

If you do not see visible improvement within your community, the person you elected is not doing their job. We elect people to act in the place of the average citizen, to attempt change in many different things. That's the job of elected officials and why we voted for them. Any official who abdicates his responsibility in order to gain financial wealth for himself is a fraud, and the rights of the community suffer.

31

In the early 1980s, the Los Angeles County Democratic Party included one of the most powerful Democrats—a Black Democrat—in the United States, Tom Bradley. In the early 1980s, Mayor Bradley was considered a possible vice presidential choice for the Democratic presidential ticket. During Bradley's twenty-year tenure as mayor of Los Angeles, his crowning accomplishment was the 1992 riots in South Central. In my opinion, this was the only memorable thing Mayor Bradley accomplished for South Central during his tenure.

No group is provided less information about the political process than Black America. No group is in more need of information about the political process than Black America. The political process and the introduction of new laws regarding crime have a greater impact upon Black America than on any other group in America. They were unaware of the major changes in the law that would have a major effect upon them and their children until it was too late. Like a tornado coming to town when no one's heard the weather report.

This is the effect of a lack of Black press. It is clear the responsibility for this lies in the lack of media and a lack of integrity by those who are elected to represent the Black community. Before Bradley became mayor, he spent more than twenty-five years with the Los Angeles Police Department. During Bradley's twenty years as mayor, police brutality did not decrease. Police brutality and abuses continued to run rampant in South Central during Bradley's administration.

As a former policeman, Bradley was well aware of the behavior going on within the LAPD. Although the mayor was quite familiar with the problem between police and citizens of South

Central, he failed to take any tangible steps to correct the problem before it became a cause of civil disobedience.

During his term as mayor, I believe and will let the record show he spent very little time addressing the police department's policing of Black communities. He merely represented a Black face for the community to be proud of, and that was enough to get Black votes.

My criticism of the Democratic Party is not meant to indicate support for any other party. Drugs and drug enforcement have been a major problem in the Black community because of the number of people it criminalizes and causes to be incarcerated. The human damage being done by this drug epidemic was fundamentally ignored. But the Democratic Party, which Black communities in the United States continually vote for, solves this by incarcerating more people without dealing with the issue of demand for such drugs within the US or giving treatment to those who are addicted.

It is only fair to point out that the most outspoken critics of the drug war were George Shultz, former secretary of state under Ronald Reagan, and William F. Buckley Jr., the conservative Republican writer. They both proposed, as early as the 1970s, the decriminalization of drugs in order to reduce the price and thereby limit the funds that were available to gangs creating havoc within Black communities. Since these drugs were being demanded by millions of American citizens, their demands would be met either legally or illegally.

This was the basic thinking behind Prohibition in the 1930s. It turned out to be a total failure, and laws were changed. Now with the actions of enforcing the law predominantly

33

against Black people, there is no need to change the law until once again drug enforcement will become so expensive and disruptive to society that the law must be changed. You've seen the beginning of changes as various states have made marijuana legal for both medicinal and personal consumption. Decriminalization differs from legalization. I do not claim to have the answers for decriminalization, but we must at least start a dialogue.

Though the Democratic Party still claims it has the best interests of minorities and the downtrodden at its heart, I see that's not true. They are simply liars. They are lying about being concerned about the underprivileged. They are lying about being concerned about those that have been disenfranchised. Conversation is not the same as action. Action speaks louder than words.

My problem was being Black and going against the powerful Democratic Party. The party controls Black politicians to the point where they are little more than lapdogs for the larger organization. The ability of the Democratic Party to limit the constitutional rights of Black America was further evidence of the need for our continued assault against them in the matter of seeking to own media controlled by the community. We were pursuing the right and the ability to provide the communications through cable television systems. They had forgotten about civil rights now that they were being inconvenienced by them. The Democratic Party view was that civil rights were okay as long as they did not inconvenience the party.

The underhanded and duplicitous treatment of Bernie Sanders during the 2016 presidential primaries and presidential cycle by Hillary Clinton and the leadership of the Democratic National

Committee, including its chairperson, is one example of the party's willingness to utilize power without regard to rules or regulations. The chairperson, Debbie Wasserman Schultz, was forced to resign when the dirty treatment became public. She is still a member of the United States Congress. Integrity is not a requirement there. If they will do that to Sanders, a senator, what will they do to Black people?

The final attempt to get outside government intervention to protect us from this treatment by the City of Los Angeles was contacting the office of John Van de Kamp, the attorney general of the State of California. Political corruption, as there was in the case of South Central, was something we thought should be brought to the attention of law enforcement authorities and the attorney general, as a leader of what gets prosecuted within the state. The attorney general was also a Democrat and was obviously reluctant to investigate or prosecute criminal behavior going on in Los Angeles. After notifying the attorney general of what we considered political corruption during our South Central licensing process, we never heard back. After the attorney general refused to investigate our charges and complaints, we contacted the FBI in our final potential resolution of the corruption.

This is where the First Amendment and the freedom of the press become important. When we were met with silence by elected officials, we could not communicate with an entire community of five hundred thousand people without the ability to utilize the very media we had been prohibited from using.

How is the effect any different than a racist judge in Mississippi? It isn't; it is worse. When the courts provide protection against constitutional violations in Mississippi, all the Black politicians want to jump on the bandwagon and support these issues. When it comes to Black and Democratic politicians stealing the rights of Black America, no one seems to care, which is part of the hypocrisy of the Democratic Party and the Black citizens voting for them. This is also why the Democratic Party is so adamant about making sure Black America cannot exercise the constitutional rights guaranteed to them.

One of the key elements of Black leadership is that they are fearful of anyone who does not fear them. Their power is not their own, but is the power of the powerful Democratic Party that controls a substantial portion of the politics in the United States. It seems Black leadership has somehow determined to continue this association from some sort of loyalty and to simply follow the party line and be rewarded without requesting any form of explanation. I believe they feel no responsibility to the average citizen whatsoever. Black politicians have plenty of rhetoric but little action.

Black politicians move from office to office and claim to be representing the public's interest as "civil servants." They are no more civil servants than the guy who robs the bank in the afternoon. They are stealing, and stealing on a big level. The politician is robbing those who have nothing, and nothing can be lower than robbing the poor. Under either scenario, the average citizen has no gain in the transaction.

Where do the media fit in? The fact is Black America does not choose its own leaders. These leaders are chosen by media that identify those they quote as civil rights leaders. What do we really know about those who call themselves our civil rights leaders? The most identifiable Black "leaders" are media-chosen civil rights leaders like Jesse Jackson, who has been a media darling

36

since the 1960s, or Al Sharpton. What tangible action have these men made recently to improve the lot of Black America other than to fly in, have a photo op, and support the policies of the Democratic Party?

People cannot determine what is best for themselves when the leadership supposedly leading them is not fully and completely known by them. People get to be successful Democratic politicians by following the instructions of the Democratic Party, supporting the principles of the Democratic Party. What these principles are I'm at a loss to tell you, except they are the hackneyed promises of forty years ago. They do not appear to be much different than those of the Republican Party: the support of the rich and the pretense they are doing something beneficial for the average American.

Who actually selects Black leadership? I know, we, the Black citizens, go to the polls and vote for whomever the Democrats put up every year. But we know so little about these people. The average citizen has no idea who their representative is in the government under which they live. All we know are the promises given every two, four, and six years. Black citizens do not have any understanding of how the system works or what they should expect from those who are supposedly leading them. This is another reason for an independent and Black-owned media.

Black leadership is selected by the media and by the Democratic Party. They will pretty much follow the party line and not be concerned about the effect their actions have upon the people in their districts and communities. There is widespread ignorance of the candidates and who they really are in the South Central community because there is no media that focuses on that community and its needs. So Black people vote for Black candidates who are the sons, daughters, families, or friends of the candidate they lovingly recall from the days of civil rights. And nothing gets done for the Black community.

I understand this is a representative democracy and we must elect our leaders according to the policies of the electorate. But we must be more discriminating with our votes and financial support of those who do not benefit our community. Examine the treatment given to big contributors for the party and the treatment received by the regular party voter. The outdated two-party system has clearly failed Black America.

The deprivation of rights did not only exist within Los Angeles but in every urban minority area in Los Angeles County. These include the cities of Compton and Inglewood and the unincorporated areas of Los Angeles County that are predominantly minority. All these areas have one thing in common: they are all controlled by the Democratic Party. All these small cities and communities and unincorporated areas were contiguous to Los Angeles and, oftentimes, were completely surrounded by the city of Los Angeles. The cities in these contiguous areas were smaller but had the same basic issues and concerns the South Central community had. The majority of the community, like most communities, were middle-income families.

These cities and communities, Black-controlled and with a majority Black population, would all fight for the civil rights accorded under the Bill of Rights to provide a free press. However, they would also join together to deny technology access to the poorest and most impoverished communities within the City and County of Los Angeles. But in my opinion, since Black politicians from three separate jurisdictions were more than willing to lock out a Black company in a new industry, we have to seriously question any leadership qualities they claim to possess. Being a sheep-like follower is not a leadership quality.

The results were deadly. By fighting against cable television, which was the new media form in the market, and prohibiting competition within the cable television industry, the city was able to limit free press. Look at the dominant news channels that provide information to the nation as a whole. You'll see they are based on cable television. News networks such as Cable News Network and Fox News were created to deliver their product directly to cable television. New media did in fact develop new press. Only Black America was excluded from the free press created by this new technology.

There was a Congressional Black Caucus (CBC) in 1986. The case of *City of Los Angeles v. Preferred Communications* clearly dealt with civil rights issues affecting African-Americans in the South Central area of Los Angeles and should have been of great importance to them. What was the position of the CBC to the case being heard by the US Supreme Court? Civil rights cases heard by the Supreme Court have an effect on all parts of the United States, including any areas represented by the members of the CBC. They did nothing, as they always do, for the protection of Black citizens. The behavior in this major civil rights case showed the CBC to be impotent and uncaring.

The CBC ignored major civil rights rulings that would have an effect on Los Angeles media and, in turn, all of Black America media for the next forty years. They should not claim to be legitimate spokespeople or representatives for the people if they do not comment on the most basic of governmental functions. The effect upon an entire community, the Black community throughout America, was ignored. What kind of functioning body whose purpose is to serve the Black community would ignore the highest court's decision about civil rights in media? This is the community they said they would represent and protect.

In my opinion, the Democratic Party uses Black politicians and Black judges to take the rights of Black citizens because if they used White judges and White politicians everyone would scream racism, which it might be, and the activities would be obvious to all. It is still racism as is, only it's Black racism. The effect is the same upon the community—they lose their rights and the ability to participate within society. Somehow there is the inclination to believe Black politicians are actually looking out for Black people. Nothing could be further from the truth. That is like saying the notorious Crips gang is looking out for the Black community because the members are Black.

I could give you a series of statistics supporting the claim that Black America is worse off now than it was forty years ago. All statistics clearly point to this conclusion. Black people are worse off during good times and bad times, because when the times are good, politicians are looking out for themselves, and when the times are bad, politicians are looking out for themselves.

Black politicians have continued to prosper, and the Black community has continued to get betrayed. Those being betrayed rarely have the ability to defend themselves. The same people hold elected office now—where they've been for the last thirty years. The office may be different, but the politicians are the same people. They did not grow integrity by changing offices.

Black politicians have prevented numerous minority businesses from entering lucrative fields they are legally entitled to enter. In addition to cable television, real estate development, transportation, and government contracts have been denied by Black political clout. They prevented Black business development through overt and covert actions. Black politicians seek to keep those who have elected them in ignorance of their actual behavior.

By blocking information necessary to make good community decisions, they have effectively blocked the ability of citizens to oversee the politicians who claim to represent them. Black politicians make it clear, when you meet them, that if you want to do any business in which they have any degree of influence, you had better pay them or some substitute person or surrogate they designate. But aren't you disrespecting the very rights for which you are fighting and the office they represent if you have to pay off politicians for their influence? If you accept that sort of treatment, they will believe such treatment is appropriate. Every dog has his day.

In my experience, local politicians are used to getting their way and being paid in some form or fashion through business opportunities that have some influence in their own districts. So the power to economically affect an entire community is in the hands of politicians who believe they have control over everything within their community. These elected officials have very little, if any, clue about the concept of economics if it doesn't line their own pockets in some way. After attempting to hold discussions with elected officials, it became clear they were clueless about how the economy, or media, truly worked.

The elected officials and their deputies gave the impression of being high school bullies. They demanded financial compensation because of the power of their office and vote. My only surprise was that they did not try to conceal their demands, which I thought illegal.

They control real estate development, and now South Central Los Angeles has a housing shortage. Is this shortage because of politicians and their policies? Cable television was different from real estate, because cable television had the protection of the United States Constitution and the Bill of Rights. This gave my partners and me the strength to continue to push forward with the ideas we had identified through our paperwork, actions, and financing with them since 1980.

Politicians now move between offices at the local, state, and federal level in order to maximize their ability to stay in power and to maintain the lucrative benefits of being a public servant. We now have professional politicians, not public servants. Most states and local communities have rightfully imposed term limits for elected politicians because of the fear that they will continue to dominate for an unlimited amount of time if left unchecked. But they go on to lateral or higher public offices, like the Peter Principle for civil servants in which people are said to rise to their level of incompetence.

Let's look at some Black elected officials and follow their path through the various offices they have held. Remember, term limits at the federal level cannot be accomplished without an amendment to the US Constitution.

I have selected this small group because it represents a cross section of Black elected officials from the Democratic Party and various governmental entities. Mark Ridley-Thomas is a supervisor for the County of Los Angeles. Los Angeles county supervisor is often called the second most powerful job in the State of California. He was a member of the Los Angeles City Council from 1991 to 2002. During his time as a Los Angeles city councilman he opposed the constitutional rights of the citizens of South Central by supporting the city's deprivation of those rights, including the Preferred Communications effort. His signature is part of the process showing the laws and recommendations from the Council. From 2002 through 2008, Ridley-Thomas was a member of the California State Assembly and State Senate. He has been a county supervisor since 2008, but term limits restricted his ability to continue in the supervisor position. Now, he is once again running for city council in Los Angeles.

Ridley-Thomas helped his son, Sebastian Ridley-Thomas, get elected to the California Senate in a special election in 2013 at the age of twenty-six. According to the *LA Times*, Sebastian Ridley-Thomas was forced to resign from the California Assembly in 2017 as he faced an investigation for sexual harassment charges. After resigning from the Assembly, he was hired as a professor at the University of Southern California (USC). After six months at USC, Sebastian Ridley-Thomas was fired after the university discovered that a $100,000 donation had been made to a program affiliated with his employment at the university. The gift ended up in the account of a nonprofit organization known as the Policy, Research, and Practice Initiative. This nonprofit was run by Sebastian Ridley-Thomas. The donation had been made from a campaign fund controlled by his father. USC requested an FBI investigation into the hiring of the younger Ridley-Thomas and the donation from his father's campaign fund.

43

In my opinion, and the opinion of many, a professional politician is a person who makes a profit from controlling your rights. I am not talking about a government paycheck. The constitutional rights of Black America are used by elected officials to provide unlawful financial gain for themselves, their families, and their friends. The misery caused by the deprivation of these rights, by those who are supposedly representing a community, is illustrated in the deprivation of technology access brought about by these local professional Black politicians. This betrayal has left a trail of long-term and devastating effects prohibiting the involvement of Black America within the larger economic order and communications of society.

Another example: Maxine Waters was first elected to the California State Assembly in 1976. Before that time, Maxine had been chief deputy for David Cunningham, a Los Angeles city councilman, prior to her becoming a member of the California State Assembly. Councilman Cunningham, of course a Black Democrat, was the deciding vote to deny Black companies the ability to provide cable television service for the South Central community. Small world, isn't it? It certainly is in Black Democratic politics.

In 1991, Waters became a member of the US House of Representatives, and she remains in that position today. Waters, the most recognizable elected official representing South Central Los Angeles, has represented the area in one elected capacity or another since 1976. In her more than forty-five years in various elected offices, nothing has changed in South Central for the better. While her name and interviews have garnered national news coverage, the people of South Central continue to get betrayed.

44

When my partners and I approached her, Waters made it quite clear that our constitutional rights did not affect her because she was a politician and part of the Democratic Party, and that's where her allegiances lie. Not with the community or Black businesses, not even to gain media status. When we first approached her, we did not know her history with Councilman Cunningham and the Los Angeles City Council. We spoke to her when she was in the California State Assembly about the importance of cable television and its influence within the community. We told her about the great possibilities for community improvement that came with the new technology. Waters replied, "This is city business that does not affect me." The willingness of elected officials to dismiss such an important industry negates the importance of it to their communities, and overlooks the behavior and unconstitutional regulations by local governments in their state—a sign all political people were part of one group. They ignored us and impeded us at every step.

On several occasions we met with Mervyn Dymally, who was the former lieutenant governor of California. Dymally would go on to become a member of the US House of Representatives, representing part of the South Central area from 1981 to 1993. At the time we spoke with Dymally, he was a member of Congress. To some extent, Dymally was more interested in our situation than other politicians. It was brought to our attention that Dymally and Tom Bradley were longtime adversaries and not on very good terms. Dymally told us he could not do anything because Bradley was so powerful within the Democratic Party.

Federal elected officials did not think the Constitution important enough to warrant their concern. Obviously their oath of office meant very little to them after they were elected.

Black leaders are not a conduit but an impediment—an elected roadblock. The behavior of Black politicians shows the rest of the government, on all levels, that it is okay to disrespect the Black community because their elected officials are going to ignore them anyway—until election time comes around.

Part of the job of a Black politician, or any politician, is to ensure the interface between Black citizens and the government is carried out fairly and equitably. The government itself can only be approachable if the representatives of the citizens and the community provide a true, clear conduit for the citizen to interface with the government.

Once again, I think the term *public servant* is a misnomer. It is clear to me, as a Black American, that those who are elected officials have little intention of providing any service to the general public. No one comes out of elected office poorer than when they went in.

Politicians' lack of ethics is an important factor in the low participation in the overall capitalist system in this country by Black Americans. There are plenty of capable people who have the ability to develop substantial businesses and are desirous of participating but are excluded by the actions and inactions of those who are supposed to be leading us.

When you are locked out of the economic system, you're locked out of the American dream—which seems to be the fate of Black America. This fate has been brought about with the express consent and assistance of many Black politicians throughout the United States, as they betray Black citizens. The price has been paid by minority communities all across the United States.

There's more to the story. When politicians leave elected office, they are appointed to various committees, boards, and commissions, allowing them to receive compensation and salaries, again under the guise of public service. How generous they all are. Sometimes, politicians become lobbyists or attorneys after they leave public office, and then they represent a system that is bought and paid for by major corporations. Is it any wonder we have such great problems within the Black community? We have no effective and positive interface with the government.

In my opinion, Black politicians recognize this possible bonanza and know providing information to the media for Black America would be to their detriment. If the community became aware of the political behavior causing many of the problems within the Black community, their citizens would become enraged.

Among other major issues is investment of capital within Black communities. In my time dealing with this issue, Black politicians took every step to prevent any major investment within the community if they did not have control over it. The ability of individual citizens to make investments within communities is what makes America strong and makes communities strong. Black politicians did not want strong Black communities; rather, they want to keep them ignorant and asking for handouts on a continuous basis. Handouts equal payback and payback equals votes. This also goes from the top down: if you, as a politician, want help from your party getting seats on committees to getting help with reelection, it's important for the national Democratic Party to maintain control of Black politicians because this gives the look of legitimacy to the Democratic Party and the candidates running on a state and national level.

The vacuum left by the lack of political leadership has opened the door for gang expansion and recruitment. Since there's no economic base for young people to get jobs, young people cannot get jobs and therefore feel the laws do not apply equally to all citizens, and the government, which is in control, doesn't serve people of color. So they look for alternatives, which are the illegal ones left to flourish in Black neighborhoods. It would be unrealistic to expect people to put trust in the government that continually violates or mangles their constitutional rights. One of the alternatives in inner-city communities is gangs.

Gangs are part of the economic order in inner-city and low-income communities. They often provide the employment that residents within the community do not feel is available to them in minority neighborhoods. Gangs give a false sense of order and personhood to the community that local governments are not willing or able to provide. This is an illusion children and teenagers get because they see the power of gangs on a continual basis. They see the power of the city, through arrests in violation of their rights, only as it destroys their lives and does nothing to benefit them. They are left to participate in the allure of potentially deadly gangs. This is not much of a choice for our youth.

In my view, the majority of Black politicians are little more than traitors to the Black community and Black youth. A traitor is defined in a dictionary as "one who betrays another's trust or is false to an obligation or duty." Synonyms to substitute for traitor are backstabber, double-crosser, double-dealer and two-timer, just to mention a few. It is not a word used in a complimentary fashion under any conditions, but rather a word indicating low moral values.

48

My partners and I had spoken with the leaders of all major civil rights organizations, including the NAACP, the Urban League, and the ACLU, and we made sure they were informed of the circumstances where our rights in the Preferred Communications case were being denied. At one point the president of the Los Angeles Urban League, John Mack, was a member of a minority organization that had sought the license we were seeking. Mack was friends with Tom Bradley and subsequently left the company trying to bring minority ownership into South Central because of pressure from Bradley.

It became clear to me that political parties, their politicians, and civil rights organizations pledged to protect Black America were no longer concerned with the civil rights guaranteed under the Constitution. They seemed to be more concerned about their allegiance and support of the Democratic Party, which paid their way and provided contributions for their activities. This represented a wholesale sellout of an entire Black community. The same sellout spread around the country in smaller cities controlled by the Democratic Party and with Black politicians as fronts in positions of authority.

As I see it, these so-called civil rights organizations, including the NAACP, the Urban League, and the ACLU, are little more than Democratic Party fronts. These fronts are designed to give the image and impression someone actually cares in the Democratic Party about poor and minority citizens. But it's a mirage.

It is a shame Black politicians who have benefited from many Supreme Court rulings now decide to disregard such rulings. It appears that those who represent the Black community are still willing to allow the loss of the civil rights of an entire community and an entire race in order to make a little extra money for themselves or their political campaigns.

In sports, when a team is being led by a coach or manager and that team continually fails, you get rid of the manager. You do not get rid of the entire team any more than you would rid this country of all Black Americans because of significant problems in the Black community. It is quite clear we, as Black Americans, must get rid of current leadership, which has been ineffective and is leading us in the wrong direction. As one tragic example stated earlier, substantial parts of our youth are incarcerated on a disproportionate and unfair basis. This is failure, not leadership.

When a corporation starts losing money and its operations start to fail in comparison with other companies within that industry, the leadership of that company is generally changed. The board of directors will change the officers who operate the company and will reestablish the opportunity for the company to participate profitably within its industry.

It is time for Black America to make a change in its leadership because our leadership has failed us. The evidence of the failure is contained in the statistics that represent Black America's overall involvement in the economy, criminal justice system, and education system. One in four Black Americans lives below the poverty line. That is the highest poverty rate of almost any group in the United States. When your leadership cannot even lead you out of poverty, they really stink. All the elected officials seem to make money while being public servants; maybe that's why so many people remain in poverty.

The supposed integrity of Black politicians is nonexistent. Not a single Black politician took a position in support of the positive civil rights ruling by the US Supreme Court in our case. Civil rights did not seem to be important when their allegiance is not to Black Americans. Their goal is allegiance to the Democratic Party.

There is a new scam in town. The newest scam being pushed by Black politicians is reparations. Are we as a race of people gullible enough to believe society is somehow going to pay reparations for events that happened five or six generations ago? If we go a step further, whose money will pay the reparations for the damage done to the citizens of South Central by the City of Los Angeles over the last forty years? That is a much more current and relevant issue that is simply being ignored by Black politicians because of their involvement and cover-up of the important issues related to this matter. If it is paid with tax money (and I pay taxes), do I have to pay my own reparations?

I recently read about a Black congresswoman, a member of the CBC, who proposed the payment of reparations to descendants of slaves. The concept indicates we are still seeking reparations 150 years later for slavery. This does not make sense in light of the fact that it is not going to happen—in my opinion, of course. I have personally been hearing about reparations from politicians for more than fifty years. The potential logistics of trying to distribute reparations for something that happened hundreds of years ago are ridiculous.

I believe this is all a red herring. The politicians will crow, "Look what I'm trying to get for you," but just like in the *Wizard of Oz*, don't look behind the curtain. The idea of the rest of America distributing this kind of payment to Black America

51

is laughable. Members of the Democratic Party simply seek to confuse the Black electorate because they also realize this is not going to happen. The discussion of reparations at the congressional level by leading Black politicians merely indicates they are seeking to subvert the attention of poor and minority communities. This is little more than a flimsy pretense of such reparation payment being possible.

They know, you know, and I know it is not going to happen. But it's good for glad-handing their constituents, gaining dollars for their campaigns, or giving the impression they are doing something. They get people excited about something that has no possible chance of happening or changing anyone's life in any way. This merely serves as a distraction from the lack of performance by those in power. How about a good paying job in the community, a much safer community, and moves to cure the drug addicted instead?

Our representatives, the elected politicians, are supposed to be looking out for our best interest. Their inability to produce valid solutions for the problems that plague our communities is a demonstration of their powerlessness to deal with the issues plaguing us. It's clear we must get rid of them and find new liaisons with the government that will represent our best interest.

When the actions do not correspond with the professed political beliefs of a party, you must decide if that party is truthful and therefore deserves your support. President Dwight Eisenhower said, "The supreme quality of leadership is integrity." Eisenhower was a US Army general in WWII before becoming president of the United States. He might know a little something about leadership.

We must have a serious examination of the leadership that has brought us to this point. Let us not dispute the fact that Black America is suffering. The question remains, will we depend upon those who put us in this hole to know how to get us out of the same hole now? I think not. I think we need a new direction with new leadership for Black America. The leadership does not necessarily have to be political, but there will be a political component to it because that is the nature of America.

We must face the difficult situation we are in. We must make difficult but necessary decisions. James Baldwin said, "Not everything that is faced can be changed, but nothing can be changed until it is faced."

Chapter 3

OF CIVIL RIGHTS, CIVIL DISOBEDIENCE, AND TYRANNY

The history of America includes the history of Black America. Both the Emancipation Proclamation by Abraham Lincoln and the "I Have a Dream" speech by Martin Luther King Jr. are an integral part of both histories. Our history as a country provides a basis for our liberty and protection in the US Constitution.

Shortly after the ratification of the Constitution the United States, the framers of the Constitution created what was known as the Bill of Rights. The Bills of Rights contains the first ten amendments to the US Constitution. The purpose of the Bill of Rights was to protect citizens from governments that exceeded their authority. It is not to protect the government from citizens. The government has an armed police force to do that. It is not an accident the First Amendment to the Bill of Rights is the right to free speech, which allows you to petition government for a redress of their offenses. All governments are supposed to comply with these rules. If any government does not comply with the Bill of Rights as established by the Constitution, there is a question as to whether such a government is valid or tyrannical.

The First Amendment states: "Congress shall make no law respecting an establishment of religion, or prohibiting the free exercise thereof; or abridging the freedom of speech, or of the press; or the right of the people peaceably to assemble, and to petition the government for a redress of grievances."

The First Amendment is often described as the most important part of the Bill of Rights. The First Amendment protects five of the most basic liberties that are available in our society: freedom of religion, freedom of speech, freedom of the press, freedom of assembly, and freedom to petition the government to correct wrongs that are perpetrated by that government. I want you to see the case of *Preferred Communications* through "First Amendment eyes" and see how the rights of South Central citizens were ignored.

The deprivation of my and my partners' First Amendment rights was caused by restricting the ability of minority investors in South Central to create cable television systems that served the communities they represented. The partners of Preferred Communications, as any other company using capital/money in a capitalist society, wanted to invest to provide cable television service to the South Central community. But we were unlawfully restricted by city and county officials, some of whom were elected and others who were city and county employees. In this way, the benefits of investing within our own community were also stolen—from us and others not in compliance with the unlawful demands of those elected officials and employees, in defiance of our First Amendment rights.

Restricting capital limits the ability of any community to grow and provide the goods and services necessary for that community. Since this decades-long behavior goes on all across the country, in urban and minority communities, it once again falls upon the leadership, the Democratic Party, to accept responsibility for its behavior and for the results of its actions. The Democratic Party leaders pick and choose, at their discretion and personal enrichment, who can invest in a community and who can't. Can this be the best way to run a community?

First Amendment rights for the cable television industry were quashed on a national level as well. When the cable television industry threatened to not carry existing broadcast stations, it became subject to legislation. Special laws were passed by Congress forcing cable television owners to carry broadcast stations. The law was subsequently changed to force them to pay the stations they now were forced to carry.

When the internet was developed in the 1990s, Black America, like most of society, could not access the market because of government interference. The internet created competition for the cable television industry. While the inability to obtain a then costly computer would eliminate your ability to access the internet, cable television had the ability to develop a portal to utilize and access the internet—without a computer. The cable television industry chose not to provide this service because they could not understand its profitability; it was principally low-income and minority communities that would need the service. Internet access is still restricted in communities where individuals cannot afford a computer, thus Black America is again denied access to technology and a portal to economic enrichment. This decision directly affects Black America, as 25 percent of Black citizens live below poverty level. No internet, no access.

The purpose of the Bill of Rights is to guarantee that all citizens are treated on an equal basis in terms of government actions. There is little doubt about the existence of gross injustices heaped upon minority citizens in Los Angeles for decades and decades. When services and technologies available to the rest of society are denied to minority communities, the minority communities must, by definition, achieve less success than those who have the higher tools of learning and education. Can any child or adult learner rightfully be denied access to the tools of technology?

You may say the government is only taking a small part of their civil rights away by denying technological opportunities, but once you start taking away a group's civil rights, it's a slippery slope. In our case, in standing up for the citizens of South Central, we were not protected by a unanimous decision from the United States Supreme Court. The political corruption and judicial malfeasance allowed the "system" to deny us and our case of our rights—a cable license to serve the people of South Central Los Angeles. This in turn echoes the systemic deprivation of rights for minority citizens, which leads to distrust of the government and little expectation Black citizens will be protected by local governments. Why would the citizens of South Central believe any of their civil rights are protected when in fact their First Amendment rights have been ripped away from them?

And who or what is the press? The press is an entity that controls media, which disseminates information to be delivered to the public. The press includes any organization that controls a tangible information delivery vehicle, such as newspapers, cable television, and digital platforms. The denial of ownership or influence on media, which has evolved to become the bulk of the twenty-first-century press, is a direct affront to the Constitution by limiting access to who can create information entities. There is no doubt in my mind that at the time we sought to create a new cable system, these systems were effectively overtaking print to becoming the press of the United States. The power of video media is clearly greater than the waning ability of print media such as newspapers to deliver messages to their intended audiences.

Because of its ability to disseminate information, media are an increasingly large factor in determining the leadership of any group of people in America. With the dominance of such media, it is not possible to compete in the political marketplace without substantial sums of money or influence to acquire media time. The people who control the media or have substantial power determine what viewers get to know or how they understand what they're told. Media are paid for heavily by political parties who become the leading advertisers during any election cycle. Who determines the news you get? Is it fake news or real news? I know that they both exist.

Media also determine what may be said about any group of people within the society. This is evidenced by the fact media have allowed the use of the N-word by Black people but not by White people. No other race speaks in such derogatory terms about themselves. The complete and total disrespect shown to Black women in modern music seems disgraceful to many. You will not see such total disrespect of any other group of women in the United States to the extent Black women are disrespected by members of their own race. As long as media companies continue to make money through the denigration of Black men and Black women, they will continue such behavior. The inability of any community to promote opposing positive values and ethics, which are beneficial to the community, limits the ability to have control over other factors such as education. Without your civil rights you cannot fully participate in the American system of government.

What we have is an industry, cable television, that was allowed to build in areas under local government licenses throughout the United States and became protected by these local governments as well. This process excluded citizen input, contrary to the Constitution of the United States. I believe these actions would be classified as an illegal protection racket if local and federal governments weren't the ones doing these things. Government officials seem to have little concern about legality as they perform their functions these days. This is the definition of tyranny.

Local governments, like the City of Los Angeles, created these cable media monopolies. Why would a government want to create a monopoly in the media? Perhaps they are trying to protect their own corruption or their own singular point of view. They would need to make sure a powerful independent media wasn't available to evaluate and report on their behavior. Under a monopoly, any reports of the true behavior going on in local government facilities could be quashed. Another reason the government might want a monopoly on the media within their cities would be to hide local government injustices, taking advantage of citizens and benefiting the elected officials and their friends. Before cable television came into the marketplace, regular television was already compromised because of the advertising dollars from political campaigns.

When you do not have open and free information in any media, you have no alternative but to accept what the media broadcast to you. Black Americans living in poverty do not need more entertainment; they need more substantive education and information to allow them to improve their lives and deal with the medical, financial, and legal issues disproportionately affecting Black America today.

Little specific information is provided within the media in regard to the negative issues affecting the Black community in a devastating way. Many of these issues could be reduced if proper education was provided and if the media would publicize these issues to bring about change. The Black community is generally ignored by the media. Most media companies try to find low-cost and low-effort solutions by presenting Black faces on the television without dealing meaningfully with Black issues. Their goal is profit, and if you cannot show them the profit from the programming, they will not likely continue to provide it.

The owners of powerful media don't want to "rock the boat" and uncover information against or create controversy with the local governments holding their licenses. Licenses for particular areas, especially minority areas, were likely given to political cronies and large political contributors. Do "friends" usually unmask friends?

In South Central there was a higher level of illiteracy and lower reading rates than in other parts of the city. The increasing effects and power of cable television became even more magnified at the beginning of the 1980s when we applied for the license forward to today. Cable television offered the opportunity for additional learning, outside the school system. These additional learning opportunities from the public channels included with local cable licenses could have provided a chance for those students who were being left behind by the school system of Los Angeles. Those who could not read or had trouble reading would be able to get the most current news through their home television, local to their needs and community. This new technology could have provided a strong incentive for development and improvement within low-income and minority communities. We tried to bring such programming through our efforts to get our South Central Los Angeles cable license. We were denied. Instead, the technology was restricted to the uses determined by political friends of elected officials of the city and county of Los Angeles. The results speak for themselves, and they are not good.

The twentieth century saw the great expansion and development of mass media. As cable television became a greater power in the media industry, the decline of newspapers and magazines had begun. The local newspaper continued its decline in both circulation and impact over the next twenty-five years. The diversity of the newspaper media was not replaced by diversity in cable television because many cities, including Los Angeles, limited access to the "new press."

The effect of mass media was to put the power of free speech in the hands of the few that had the political connections necessary to influence and acquire access to media. So media ownership was restricted to people with political connections who didn't need any experience or capital to get involved in the business. Electronic media were siphoned through and required to meet the political approval of a government in order to allow our investment group, and by proxy, South Central Los Angeles, to exercise our First Amendment rights. Though the public rights-of-way were large, the number of cable companies allowed to go into business were very small in comparison. Today, after mergers, they are even smaller in number and more powerful. This access to media in minority areas was reserved for powerful members of the Democratic Party, their friends, and large contributors to the party. People would now receive information from the electronic media installed into their houses, media that were controlled by government-protected monopolies they had no control over.

The government has had control of media since the inception of electronic mass media, including radio and television, the original major forms of over-the-air mass communication in the United States. Gaining a cable television license presented two opportunities. First, cable television presented a unique opportunity for ownership of mass media by minorities. Second, federal control of media was reduced due to cable television's ability to use local public right-of-way as opposed to over-the-air signals.

Cable television allowed for mass media to be constructed and broadcast in small parcels in a defined geographic area. In Los Angeles, there were fifteen communities that were to be served. South Central was only one of these communities. But in our case, the opportunities offered by cable television to serve this minority area were quashed by the city and county governments of Los Angeles. The Democratic Party was in major control of local governments and minority areas in Los Angeles at that time and continues to be in control today. Minorities are still continually excluded from mass media ownership opportunities. Is there a connection?

The timing of getting this new technology was critical to being informed in our ever-changing world. Cable television was to Black America what the internet would become to the rest of

America in the coming years. The changing technology would offer access to information that was previously unavailable or laboriously available to only those who had the time and the money. The new media would offer new opportunities for education of all types and communication among members within a community. The community could now decide what information it deemed relevant and important to its existence, a unique opportunity that would come around only once in a generation. It was seized upon by the citizens of other communities in Los Angeles, but was denied by the City of Los Angeles to the South Central community.

The denial of civil rights to Black America has been constant for many decades and centuries. The civil disobedience marches and protests during the 1950s and early 1960s were one of the most successful examples of civil disobedience bringing about significant change in our modern world. It was television that gave the people of the entire United States the opportunity to see the mistreatment of Black Americans by police throughout the South. These sickening images were broadcast on televisions in their homes. It was through televising these methods of nonviolent civil disobedience led by Black Americans that local and national governments began to correct behavior that was depriving Black citizens. Civil disobedience is often a reaction to tyranny.

Would you call the South from the 1920s through the 1950s tyrannical? If you would, you understand tyrants and tyranny. A tyrant is a ruler who is unrestrained by law. In the United States the Constitution is our foundational law abhorring excessively controlling rulers to the detriment of its citizens. I believe the iconic Los Angeles City Hall cannot hide the tyranny that reigns within it. Again, our cable case is only one small example.

According to *Encyclopedia Britannica*, "Racial segregation provides a means of maintaining the economic advantage of the politically dominant group." This is what was done with cable television in South Central. They segregated the population and provided only the information they deemed appropriate within the South Central community. The ability of the government to limit entrance into the marketplace and to the press was in fact an attempt to limit the rights of those who live in the South Central community. The city denied the technology only to Black people within the city. The members of the community who wished to utilize this public communication right-of-way, to speak within their own community, were denied access to the market. Would a rich contributor somehow have a concern for or knowledge of the problems and interests of South Central? Unlikely.

If this governmental behavior in our cable license case had happened in Mississippi or Alabama, it would be considered racism. Yes. This is Black-on-Black racism. This is institutional and systemic racism. This is also one of the most dangerous situations of Black-on-Black crime.

In 1980, applications were filed to obtain nonexclusive licenses to provide cable television service in the community defined as South Central Los Angeles. In 1982, more than two years after the applications were filed, the City of Los Angeles decided to throw out all applications and create a new bureaucratic department that would license only the South Central area. Creating new bureaucratic departments to handle a segregated people exclusively is an example of institutional racism. Isn't that what happened with the Jim Crow laws in the South that excluded Blacks from entering into society fully and set integration efforts back for generations?

From our standpoint, the city made it quite clear that our failure to pay a hefty bribe would result in our not being able to do business within the city of Los Angeles. The approach in seeking bribes was rather simple. You give a councilman's deputy and Mayor Bradley's friend controlling interest in your company, and you still put up the money to build the system. Since that was clearly an unacceptable approach from our standpoint, they made an offer to provide us an office building and some vacant land in downtown Los Angeles in exchange for dropping out of the race for the cable television license. We could not accept either proposal because they both appeared to be illegal. We feared law enforcement showing up at our door and asking how we had done any deal with elected officials. When the applications were summarily rejected in 1982, the final two companies remaining were said to be minority companies. One company, with no money, was composed of the political friends of Mayor Bradley and certain Black city councilmen.

The new two-year process was only the beginning of the delays the city would set in place as roadblocks to prevent the South Central area of Los Angeles from getting cable television service. Remember, there were fifteen communities needing cable television service. In 1982, when the city rejected all applications for licenses for the South Central area, the other fourteen licenses had been awarded, had already been constructed, or were being constructed. Once again, the South Central community was deprived of their basic civil rights as defined by the Constitution. The least were the last again.

Additional reasons for cable television not being provided in South Central were evident. Among these were that major companies were not interested in providing service in the South

66

Central area because they did not understand the needs of Black people and feared the level of poverty would adversely impact their potential earnings in the area considering the large amount of money they would spend sinking cable into the streets and homes of these minority customers. Black South Central citizens would have no input in the deployment of private capital within their own community.

This adverse decision to deny our license was one of many negatively affecting the South Central community. How can any group prosper when denied their mass media rights as well as their basic economic rights that go with being an American?

In 1985, the city awarded a license to operate a cable television system to a company controlled by a major Democratic contributor by the name of Eli Broad. A small part of the company was owned by the same friends of Mayor Bradley and Black councilmen who had demanded that we pay them for political access. After holding a license to construct a cable television system in South Central for more than two years, Broad's company, which owned the only license to provide cable television service in South Central, decided they did not want to go into the business of providing cable connectivity to the citizens of South Central. Broad's company had no other cable television properties. The city still refused to accept our application for a license to build a cable system in South Central. After the Supreme Court decision, this company did not want to involve itself in any competition for the market that they had been told they could monopolize.

Without ever building any cable television system or providing an inch of cable or any programming, the license awarded to Broad was sold in 1987 to a large cable television company that said it would construct a cable television system. The system built by the second company was not completed in South Central until 1990. This created a delay of ten years, a decade, in obtaining the technology available to the rest of the United States. Think of what a ten-year deferral of the deployment of essential technology would mean in the United States today. It meant even more in South Central because their resources were so limited—any benefit would have been a great benefit to this underserved community.

I contend South Central had been systematically blocked from utilizing technology that could have made substantial changes in the lives of the citizens within its community. It was clear the Los Angeles city government did not care about the needs of the community and the potential of cable television to provide services that would enhance so many neglected areas in their community. The failure to allow the poorest area of the city to have access to basic technology, readily available to other Los Angeles neighborhoods, served to exacerbate the problems that already existed within that community. All chances for the South Central Los Angeles community to improve itself through the use of technology were barred by the government. For ten years.

As the internet matured, cable television would once again have a substantial influence over delivery of internet material. The power of the internet and its influence in mass communications became known. But the companies who had monopoly control, given by elected officials and bureaucrats, were able to influence the broadband delivery system necessary for high-speed cable services. This could not have been anticipated when they were awarded their monopoly of cable licenses. Ownership of cable television systems would have allowed Black America to access the internet and reap its benefits many, many years sooner. The cable television industry evolved into broadband technology, and Black America was once again behind the curve when it came to internet technology. The lack of access to a media delivery system put minority content developers, especially Black minority developers, at a disadvantage because of the lack of outlet for their products.

Cable television offered an opportunity for a severely isolated South Central community to participate in the rest of society's progress. The isolation was both on an economic and educational level. As we know, this technology offered a vast jump in the ability of people to educate themselves with the resources they could provide within their own community from their own homes. The denial of this opportunity and the broadband speed to use the internet was another denial of First Amendment rights to the members of the South Central community to improve and educate themselves in accordance with their beliefs. It is especially important to emphasize the city and county governments of Los Angeles and their lack of independence and concern for South Central.

As I see it, when the government controls the media within a given community, it also limits the economic system that governs the community. Cable television became a major resource of information local government was able to limit, a violation of the First Amendment.

With the passage of time and lack of technology, the problems within South Central continued to increase. South Central was intentionally penalized for seeking to improve its own situation. The denial of access to technology caused by the City of Los Angeles became a terrible blow to the South Central community. Put simply, the local government made this decision and it led to the lack of improvement in South Central. Who would want that? The myriad advantages of and exposures to new technology increased elsewhere in the early 1980s; South Central Los Angeles was left behind, and the reaping of those mistakes is all too evident today.

Narrowcasting, an emerging concept unique to cable television, was also denied to the South Central community. Narrowcasting is the tailoring of content to meet a much smaller marketplace than could be done with over-the-air broadcast television. An over-the-air broadcast station could only carry one piece of programming at any one time. Conversely, cable television could carry hundreds of pieces of programming at any single time. This could have been an ideal situation for urban and minority communities who had specific educational, health, and financial needs and therefore needed programming to address these issues. This denial was just another slap in the face for South Central Los Angeles.

Cable television was an opportunity to define the critical and individual needs and information within any given community. Who is to define what is critical to your lifestyle within your community when it is so different than the remainder of the city? The important issues in Bel Air were not all that important in South Central, and vice versa. It is important for people, within their own communities, to define the important issues in that community and not allow third parties, who reside in worlds devoid of their issues, to determine what is right and appropriate for the needs of that community.

The level of change that could occur in South Central with the introduction of cable television was greater than in the rest of the city because the community had fewer resources. Inferior schools and limited access to modern technology put South Central Los Angeles behind the rest of their city and society in general. Just look at the educational test scores of other communities in Los Angeles against those of South Central Los Angeles. This technological change offered the chance to create systems and educational opportunities not currently being provided because capital investments were not being made in the infrastructure of South Central Los Angeles.

We identified programming options for the South Central community that might not have been profitable, such as parenting classes, educational programs, and information about senior health care, on our local-access channels. Others did not have an interest in making such a substantial investment within the community. Opportunities for quality content development were abundant in a city considered a content-creation capital of the world. More lost opportunities.

Change brought by cable television could make a dramatic impact on the education and information available to low-income and minority communities. The improvement of education would lead to an improvement in employment opportunities and higher education. The improvement in employment would provide an improvement in community incomes and thereby reduce the level of poverty within the community. I again contend these benefits were all denied to the lowest-income community in order for political friends of corrupt politicians to benefit personally and financially. Just look at their wealth before and after their time in political office. Their financial benefit came at the expense of everyone, especially those with the lowest incomes in the United States, who could afford such blatant disregard the least.

Such control of cable television in the early 1980s was the equivalent of the awful control of the internet today. The owners of the cable television systems had the ability to decide what information they allowed into the community they were supposed to be serving. Since companies had a monopoly, on a corporate level, sometimes thousands of miles away from the communities they served, they showed little, if any, interest in the lives of the people of South Central. This power across distance was given to them by their friends, the politicians.

By the time cable television had been installed in most minority areas in the US, they were basically ten years behind their wealthier counterparts in the Los Angeles area and the nation. The internet's influence dwarfed all other media as the twenty-first century approached.

Now let's look at the personal economics of Black America. Low incomes locked a substantial portion of minority citizens out of the internet, as they could not afford a computer and therefore access to the internet when the internet revolution began—a prohibitive expense for, say, ten years. So ten years of not having cable access for South Central and ten years from owning computers! That's twenty years. Computers became less expensive as access and reliance on personal technology devices increased. But that still doesn't excuse or change the fact that large capital investment into a cable television system could have overcome the lack of computers and given Black America access to the internet many years earlier than they received it.

The actions of the City of Los Angeles ensured Black America would never have control over media, cable, and broadband to respond to the media needs of their community. It was clear that the needs of the community were substantially different than those of other parts of society, considering the high poverty levels and the lower education levels that existed within the South Central community. The ability to transcend the issues of high poverty and low education and to spread pertinent community information could have been obtained with the proper utilization of cable television and its morphing into the internet.

No, cable television was not going to solve all the issues existing within South Central. The technology could, however, have provided a source of information to make informed decisions and education to correct some of the problems needing to be addressed. Without access to or control of media, South Central Los Angeles residents were effectively disenfranchised by the sitting city and county governments.

Black America has had little control—a few cable networks and a few shows—in the overall structure of television resources that would allow specific programming for the needs of the community. Most of the above are not tailored in any way for education and specific community needs. The community has different problems than general society, and the effects of denying technology to the community have become substantial and deadly. With the advent of the general use of television, computers, and personal information devices, parents and communities have to compete with the images projected on television for the attention and education of their children and their community in general. These images of minority citizens are rarely positive.

I believe, and research shows, that by the 1980s and 1990s television had more influence upon the growth and development of moral values in children than parents and the broader community. Substantial control over the input minority children receive has been ceded to electronic media, and thus there are few positive role models for those children in television programming. Cable television had the ability to deliver internet access without the need for a computer. But large cable companies felt this benefit would reduce their income. Each company may choose its own direction, but when you are a monopoly your direction is the only one.

Another issue facing minority communities is education. When you're denied your right to the First Amendment, you're denied your right to educate your children and to provide the moral fiber that is necessary for your children to exist and flourish within society. The government seeks to blame the parents or the community, but programming is a means of education—perhaps the wrong kind of education, information, and standards by which you want to raise your children. In my opinion, the government has blocked the use of public access rights-of-way that would allow parents to have more influence over their children's lives. Not having such influence can often lead to trouble.

This was happening at a time when many children were afraid to go to school because of the level of violence that existed within their community and because of the power of the gangs to control that community. High levels of stress are standard for children within low-income and minority communities.

The ability to exercise First Amendment rights would have given parents the ability to supplement the education being taught so poorly by the Los Angeles Unified School District (LAUSD). When you cannot educate your own children to the education standards of this country, or rely on the government-controlled state education system, you cannot expect citizens to improve their lot in life. How can they compete? They cannot compete because they do not have the skills and resources necessary to compete. What is the effect of having inferior abilities in a highly competitive marketplace? You need merely look at the inner city of any major city in the United States today and you will see the answer. There is a disproportionate occurrence of poverty, crime, and mental illness. These factors go hand in hand with lower education levels.

Freedom of the press is fundamental to the concept of freedom as a nation. Without a free press there can be no true freedom within any nation. In any situation where one nation seeks to take over another nation, some of the first things they seek to control are the press and media. The control of the press and media allows them to influence what the public believes. If you reinforce that you are a liberator, you will be considered a liberator. If the alternative view is put forth that you are an attacker, an enemy, then the public will go along with that line of thought. That is the power of the press. The ability of the press to influence the subconscious mind of citizens is unrefuted. It is hard to look at community issues, find solutions, and refute inaccurate information without a free press.

Who is the press for Black America? The fact is, there is little to no press for Black America by Black America. When you are not in control of the information being disseminated about you or your community, you are not in control of the image presented about you or your community. The Los Angeles city and county governments decided to limit access to the control of media by refusing to allow Black citizens access to cable television delivery. Since most urban areas are controlled by the Democratic Party, I can say this behavior was also that of the Democratic Party.

The lack of an effective Black press during the 1980s and 1990s meant Black America would never have the opportunity to control its own destiny. While some would like to say it is an accident, it was the plan by the Democratic Party to control the Black vote with decades of empty promises and control Black America without providing any benefits during their time in power. The effective lack of Black press continues until this very day.

This media, cable television, was being used to expand education and information opportunities throughout the United States, but cable television was being denied to the citizens of South Central Los Angeles, who needed it most. This media offered educational opportunities and information that is critical for continued existence, including medical and financial information. Remote learning was available as early as 1980 but was denied in South Central. The entertainment aspects are merely there to distract and to sell the advertising that makes owning a media monopoly very profitable.

Many things have changed from the inception of the Constitution to the current day. Technology has made a vast difference in how things are pursued and how information is distributed among the public. It is now mandatory that you have access to media for everything from entertainment to seeking peaceable redress from your grievances against government.

Not everything that comes through media is entertainment. The media are merely a delivery vehicle. You generally have the ability to give instructions as to what you want to be delivered to you. The determination of what that media deliver is controlled by those who control the media. The concept that all media are merely entertainment is both fallacious and dangerous.

The media are used to transmit news, information, and educational material as deemed appropriate by those who control that media. There is a reason why there is a freedom of the press clause in the First Amendment. News is not supposed to be merely entertainment. Its function is to provide relevant information to citizens in order that they may be capable of making informed decisions about the things going on in their community, their society, and especially their government.

In the original creation of television networks, news was a separate entity and was not at all related to the entertainment portion of a television station. As the media owners sought more and more profits from their protected position, they combined news with entertainment and the independence of news was thrown out the window for the sake of profit.

The internet was not a viable media alternative when cable television was originally created. Cable television was the dramatic change in technology that offered citizens access to information and media on a more direct basis. You have a choice of over one hundred channels with cable or six channels over the air. The majority of citizens in this country chose to go with cable because the access to additional information was not being provided by the over-the-air channels, along with new avenues of thought.

The lack of ability to access technology was a damning force for a community that had struggled with education and unemployment for many decades. Without education you cannot understand the society that we live in and how it functions. To deprive such a large number of people the ability to participate in society is a great penalty. This penalty is brought about in order to provide political and economic benefits for the friends of elected officials. This is a travesty of the justice system and a disgrace.

The inability of parents to participate in the development of children's education is a leading component of why there is less educational growth within urban and minority communities. Without access to media, a large community cannot impact the education that their children receive. We must look to ourselves and try to make sure that we are providing opportunities for those who seek opportunities, especially in education.

I am often surprised by the reaction to civil disobedience. I'm surprised that others are truly surprised about the need for civil disobedience. I am surprised that there is not more civil disobedience. The use of civil disobedience often serves as a petition to the existing government to provide fair and decent treatment to the citizens.

In my opinion, media decide which issues pervade minority communities, not the communities themselves. The concerns of minority and low-income communities are simply ignored by mainstream media, perhaps because they feel that minorities are not worthy of knowing what goes on within their own communities. When all recourse is left unavailable to the general citizenry, they sometimes seek other methods such as civil disobedience as they attempt to bring government behavior that is detrimental and dangerous to the community to the attention of the general public.

Let's be clear. There are numerous forms of civil disobedience. There are violent forms of civil disobedience and nonviolent forms. Various groups in our society now believe trying to bring your grievances to various governments is an exercise in futility. The behavior of many local governments is without regard for justice in our society today.

What's also quite clear is minorities have limited ability to petition the government to reverse its unjust behavior in regard to what it does to citizens. One important civil and constitutional right is for the public to be able to seek a peaceable method of finding solutions when the government has exceeded their legal authority. This is called seeking the right to redress. If the government can stop you from seeking legitimate redress for your grievances, they are in fact stopping the operation of the Constitution. If they are able to stop the operation of the Constitution, then we once again face tyranny. So tyranny breeds anarchy—and well-meaning and innocent people are harmed.

The rights to educate yourself and to improve your life are created in the Constitution not by senators, congressmen, or state or local officials. Civil rights must be for all persons or the concept is invalid. What is even more dangerous are those who claim to be civil rights leaders but are in fact the ones that are assisting in stealing your civil rights.

In Los Angeles, Black citizens are often segregated by the city in the provision of services that are offered. Generally you find that when the government segregates Black people, it is rarely for the benefit of those who have been segregated. In my opinion, the reason people are segregated by the government is so that they can be treated differently than those who have not been separated and deprived of things other citizens enjoy.

There are two types of segregation. The first is de facto segregation. De facto segregation is racial discrimination not mandated by law. It is brought about by individual preference, prejudice, and social norms. The Civil Rights Act of 1964 ended decades of segregation, but de facto segregation continued.

De jure segregation refers to intentional actions by the government to enforce racial segregation. The Jim Crow laws of the southern states, which endured until the 1960s, are examples of de jure segregation or discrimination upon the entire race. As an example, let's use the Supreme Court case *Brown v. Board of Education*. In 1954, the Brown family sought to send their child to a local school, the closest school to their house in Kansas, but the school did not allow Black children to attend. The Brown family sued, and the landmark case became known as *Brown v. Board of Education*. This was a case of de jure segregation in modern America—segregation by law. Thurgood Marshall argued the case successfully before the US Supreme Court as an attorney for the Brown family and later became a US Supreme Court justice.

In contrast, de facto racial segregation is accomplished by factors apart from overt or conscious government activity. These cases are not so easy to identify or fight.

It is not a surprise that South Central was the last group and area to receive cable television service in the city of Los Angeles. It is hard to believe the city professed its concern about the best interests of the community when in fact the

City of Los Angeles delayed and prevented the introduction of modern technology to minority communities.

Technology segregation was more dangerous than physical segregation because it eliminated the ability to benefit from the information sources available, which are worldwide and available from your home. By limiting the information within a given community about the technology and its ability to do transformative things within the community, the community was once again doomed by government laws that slowed their access to technology. South Central was just getting cable television when the internet became dominant—way behind other area communities. Black America had been intentionally put behind the technology curve in America.

The city attempted to justify this gross disparity by saying they were trying to do a favor for Black Americans who lived in Los Angeles. To me, the position of the City of Los Angeles was that, in areas controlled by the Democratic Party, they would decide which friends and cronies got the cable license. This is segregation established by legal governments and called de jure segregation, or segregation by law. These situations were caused by the Los Angeles County Democratic Party and the City of Los Angeles in 1986 with its Black mayor, Tom Bradley. I believe the City of Los Angeles has been enforcing Jim Crow laws in California for a long time. They're not quite as liberal as they would have you believe.

Racial segregation, in my view, is used to limit the economic ability of the segregated group. This is what was done with cable television in South Central. They segregated the population only to provide the information they deemed appropriate within the South Central community. The ability of the government to limit entrance into the marketplace and to the press was in fact an attempt to limit the rights of those who live in the South Central community. The city denied the technology only to Black people within the city.

We can also speak of deprivation in terms of the media, as the technology was being converted to a digital media platform in the United States. The assurance that minorities could not have access to digital media was an assurance that minorities would not be able to have equal access to improve their own situation in life. In over forty years, equal access to media has not been achieved in the South Central neighborhood in the city of Los Angeles, and in this most recent case of digital conversion, the city has failed South Central and not allowed them the rights guaranteed to them.

Peaceful civil disobedience was necessary during the late 1950s and the early 1960s in order to express Black America's dissatisfaction with their mistreatment. Dr. Martin Luther King Jr. led an entire change for the Black race through the use of civil disobedience. His civil disobedience took the form of nonviolent methods such as protests and marches. He was often arrested for such behavior and accepted the consequences that go with civil disobedience under a corrupt government. Television was a primary component of the ability of America to visualize the treatment that Black America had been suffering in the United States. Now that the entire world could see, there would be actual change to the treatment of Black America. The 1964 Civil Rights Act was the culmination of this extensive civil disobedience at work.

Civil disobedience is simply a refusal to comply with certain laws you believe to be unjust. A respected dictionary defines civil disobedience as "the refusal to obey governmental demands or commands especially as a nonviolent and usually collective means of forcing concession from the government." Civil disobedience is sometimes equated with peaceful protests or nonviolent resistance. The term *civil disobedience* was popularized by Henry David Thoreau in his essay "Civil Disobedience." Thoreau said in 1849 it was the responsibility and duty of the citizens to speak up in order that they not be made agents of government injustice.

Civil disobedience is often a petition for protection from government injustice when legitimate petitions are not allowed or ignored. When this is your only means of expressing yourself to the general public and to society at large, then there is a problem. Part of the problem is how civil disobedience is treated by governments that have refused to obey the Constitution. These governments are not looking out for the rights of those who are engaged in civil disobedience. Conversely, they are seeking to punish those who are engaged in civil disobedience by using law enforcement to thwart any attempt to make the position of the disenfranchised known. This behavior is more common in third world countries.

An example of a nonviolent demonstration of civil disobedience is a sit-in or people standing on the street holding signs. Riots are an example of violent protests and often use current events to justify a dangerous level of civil disobedience. It is dangerous because it involves danger to the lives of those participating in the demonstration and to those engaged in felonies such as assault and theft. Violent civil disobedience represents a danger to all members of the community. While most seek to express the concerns about government actions, some use civil disobedience to steal and loot, diminishing the message of the protest.

Civil disobedience often appears to be the only answer available to those who are disenfranchised. In America, poor and minority citizens are the most disenfranchised.

When you cannot seek a peaceful method for the redress of your grievances, you sometimes seek a violent method or any method that will allow you to express yourself so that others will know that there is a problem. The purpose of civil rights is so that all citizens would seek to be obedient to the overall rule of law. When the government refuses to comply with the law that governs it, trust is eroded. When the law is not equally applied, conflict arises.

In Los Angeles, most major events of civil disobedience have been caused by reactions to police conduct. In 1965 and 1992, the reactions of the community were based upon the actions of police, who they felt were mistreating Black citizens. It was not an isolated instance of mistreatment but rather the overall pattern of mistreatment existing within Black communities and in their relationships and encounters with the police. One event can be the catalyst for a lot of underlying fuel, such as the behavior exhibited to citizens by the police for many years.

Police brutality is clearly a reason to petition government. When any government fails to address the legitimate demands of citizens, the government has failed in its responsibility to the citizens. This is where civil disobedience starts. The failure of the government to provide equal protection to all communities was clearly happening in South Central in 1965 and 1992. This was another source of complaints by the community.

It had become clear that the police could not protect citizens of the South Central community, and therefore the citizens sought to protect themselves. Every young man in low-income and minority communities was treated as a gang member. Some persons in these communities carried guns in order to protect themselves from those who would do them harm, believing they were affiliated with one of the gangs in South Central. People became afraid of the gangs and the police, and the war zone grew.

The danger within the community also limited movement within the community, as a matter of self-protection and self-preservation. Many people were arrested and convicted for weapons violations for possessing firearms in the middle of a war zone. The choices were to deal with the police and a felony conviction or be shot dead by the gangs that ran the streets. Once again, this is not really much of a choice to have to face on a day-to-day basis.

The method of petitioning government has changed dramatically since the Constitution was created. The growth of electronic media has substantially changed the way that citizens are able to pursue their legitimate goals. The willingness of a government to ignore important issues of its citizens led to the creation of the United States.

The ongoing national campaign—in the late 1950s and the 1960s—of civil disobedience began to be covered by national news and therefore exposed the inability to seek a justifiable redress from government excesses both in the South and in the North. Since the government would not allow First Amendment rights, there was no other way except by civil disobedience to make the grievances of the community known to all those in government and the general public. Established media tend to ignore most situations regarding Black America until it becomes a crisis. It becomes a crisis when it affects the society overall and not just South Central.

The slaughter that I speak of is an economic slaughter as well as the slaughter of human beings that is partially caused by the economic slaughter. In their own communities the Black population is prohibited from participating in the economic system that governs the operation of this country. When you are excluded from the economic system, you are excluded from full participation within the overall society.

We cannot petition government if we cannot use a public right-of-way or the current technological advances. Since the City of Los Angeles has determined Black people should not have First Amendment rights and continues to enforce that outdated and illegal rule, Black people can expect more civil disobedience in the future.

In the past, minority and low-income members of the South Central community could not petition government because they were never given a fair opportunity to present the issues and problems permeating their community in ways other than going to City Hall or having community meetings without the help of media to gain public support beyond South Central. Without the ability to petition government for the rights and benefits that they are legally entitled to, the citizens of South Central find themselves permanently treated as third-class citizens. This treatment was especially true at the hands of Black politicians from the Democratic Party.

The ownership of cable television and access to the medium would allow for an opportunity to seek redress for the grievances that the government of the City of Los Angeles was heaping upon citizens of South Central.

As I mentioned before, in our *Preferred Communications* case in 1992, US District Court Judge Consuelo Marshall ruled the city had been violating the constitutional rights of our group for ten years. At the end of ten years of depriving half a million people of their constitutional rights, the city's only penalty was one dollar. The determination of damages in a civil trial is a triable issue of fact.

We were not allowed a jury trial by Judge Marshall to determine the appropriate amount of damages caused to our organization during the ten-year fight and the deprivation of our civil rights. When your most valuable rights can be acquired for a dollar, they are effectively worthless. You cannot buy a candy bar with one dollar. When the rights that protect you from the government are worthless, the government is out of control. Again, tyranny. This is the method of rule over South Central by the City of Los Angeles.

The most basic concept of law indicates that there must be penalties for the failure to abide by society's laws. No one is going to abide by any set of laws for which there is no penalty for your failure to comply. I think we all understand that if you were able to speed at your own rate, and there was no penalty for speeding, you would continue to exceed the speed limit any time you wanted to. This is more important when it comes to your civil rights as they are something that is guaranteed by the Constitution and not by any local, state, or federal government. You can imagine the chaos that would exist within society if there were no penalties for breaking laws.

The behavior of the judge in this case was chilling to all future cases and would discourage any future challenges to local government for constitutional rights; even if you were successful in proving your rights had been violated, those rights were deemed basically worthless. Rights should not be worthless.

In Judge Marshall's court, the deprivation of the constitutional rights of half a million people—for ten years—seemed of little interest to the City of Los Angeles, despite the fact that the deprived community needed resources more than any other community in Los Angeles. The fact that they were minorities meant the City of Los Angeles didn't care what happened to them or that their rights were being deprived.

Another example of political control of Black areas by the Democratic Party happened in the development of cable television in New York City. In New York City, the cable television monopoly franchise for Southeast Queens was given to a company controlled by Percy Sutton. Sutton, a prominent Democrat, was the former president of the borough of Manhattan prior to acquiring full control over all cable television in Southeast Queens, which was predominantly Black. Once again, like in South Central Los Angeles, this happened after all other areas already had cable access. The corruption of cable television in New York was so great that the Democratic borough president of Queens, Donald Manes, allegedly committed suicide rather than face the consequences of the corruption tied to his office in regard to cable television.

Cable television was allowed to operate as a monopoly with the protection of local governments. There were no adverse consequences to either the cable companies or local governments despite the fact that they were in violation of the US Constitution. The entire cable television industry was able to grow and prosper based on local governments being willing to allow the violation of the US Constitution in their jurisdictions. Cable television was not able to create its own monopoly—only the government could use its powers to create an unregulated monopoly. Cable became a prime example of corporate acquisition of local governments.

South Central is the most visible representation of what other urban areas around the United States are going through and have gone through. Their rights are being taken by local governments like the City of Los Angeles. This is what happens when people lose civil rights because they are taken by governments. The process is called tyranny.

The City of Los Angeles and a series of Black politicians seemed to do whatever was necessary to make sure the people of South Central could not exercise the rights guaranteed to them by the Constitution. What kind of city is the City of Los Angeles? It is one of the most corrupt local governments and cities in the United States but sells an image fully edited and produced by Hollywood.

Your children are at the mercy of those who provide the media that they depend upon to form opinions and values. The ability of parents to influence the power of the media is being reduced on a daily basis, especially as additional media, including the internet, spring up. This is not limited to Black America.

This monopoly was sure to have a substantial impact on the voting power that is critical to their continued political success within the electoral process. The people that I'm speaking of are the Democratic Party and the Democratic Party of the County of Los Angeles specifically. It is their power that protected those that refused to allow the citizens of South Central access to the technology. The information and the media necessary to remedy adverse conditions within their community, grow themselves, and improve their condition were illegally denied.

While the government may make many rules and regulations in order to control business, the area of cable television was no longer a dispute. The United States Supreme Court had made it clear that to allow only one company to control media within a given area was a violation of the First Amendment to the Constitution. They did exactly what they were told they could not legally do. While Black politicians like to pay great lip service to your constitutional rights, they were at the forefront of groups that were seeking to limit the rights of Black America for a profit.

Chapter 4

JUDGE AND JURY

The integrity of Black politicians must be called into serious question when they refuse to abide by the rulings of the US Supreme Court. The Supreme Court, of late, has made the rights of Black America part of the law of the nation with cases like *Brown v. Board of Education, Shelley v. Kraemer,* and *Loving v. Virginia*, to name a few. While Black politicians all over the country would always pay homage to Thurgood Marshall, the first Black Supreme Court justice, they did not honor his work or his opinion.

Justice Marshall was one of the nine Supreme Court justices who ruled in our favor against the City of Los Angeles's attempt to limit the voice of free media in South Central Los Angeles. He said the city refused to respect the civil rights of Black Americans under the First Amendment within the City of Los Angeles. The same behavior had been practiced not only in Los Angeles, but in over half the cities across the country— those controlled by the Democrats during this time.

Keeping people uneducated is one of the ways politicians protect themselves and hide their ineptitude. Lack of knowledge is very dangerous when it comes to decision-making about our elected officials. The most effective decision-makers do not cast their ballot without taking valid information into account. Black America has been denied the opportunity that exists for the entire nation under the Bill of Rights. Why? Education has long been a method to escape poverty. Freedom of the press is critical to the ability to gain the knowledge that is necessary to survive and prosper in your own community.

Elected officials are not the only ones who have been selling out Black America. Appointed officials such as US District Court Judge Consuelo Marshall have been at the forefront of making sure the civil rights of Black Americans are simply ignored by the government. She was the judge to help deny our license, to ignore a 9–0 US Supreme Court ruling, and to get away with it under the guise of Democratic Black leadership and elected officials.

There is something seriously wrong in America when the will of the United States Supreme Court is disregarded when it comes to the civil rights of Black Americans. Everybody is afraid to say anything because this judge was Black. Judges have morphed into politicians. They serve the party that appointed them. Behavior like that demonstrated by Judge Marshall is the reason for the Seventh Amendment to the Constitution.

It seems the concept of judicial independence no longer exists in Los Angeles. Our case was just one of many. The judiciary is supposed to be one of the three parts of government allowing the smooth functioning of all government. While we did not expect fair and equitable treatment from politicians, I certainly had the expectation that federal courts would comply with, and equitably follow, the rulings of higher courts. The US

Supreme Court has protected the rights of Black America for many years.

The right to receive a jury trial in civil cases is guaranteed by the Seventh Amendment to the US Constitution. As stated before, the opportunity to present the case for damages to a jury was denied by US District Court Judge Consuelo Marshall, a Black federal judge who was appointed by a Democratic president. The denial of our right to enter a multibillion-dollar industry, after a US Supreme Court decision of 9–0 in our favor, was valued at one dollar by Judge Marshall. The civil rights of more than half a million people living in the South Central community were valued at one dollar. How can anyone feel their rights have any value when they are insulted and dismissed by those who hold the power over the law? Judge Marshall allowed and assisted in the violation of our constitutional rights. When rulings such as this come from the level of a federal judge, we should all be concerned.

The right to a jury trial is one of the most treasured rights in the United States judicial system. The denial of a jury trial prohibits you from obtaining your rights and the damages from the deprivation of those rights. A jury could not have awarded less than one dollar, if we'd been able to get before a jury. The jury would also have been able to hear allegations regarding the criminal behavior that was prevalent in City Hall. The jury could have awarded tens of millions of dollars for the damage done in restraining a company from entering a multibillion-dollar industry in a major urban market. The Seventh Amendment was added to the Bill of Rights to cover situations exactly like the one we faced with Judge Marshall.

The Seventh Amendment states, "In suits at common law, where the value in controversy shall exceed twenty dollars, the right of trial by jury shall be preserved, and no fact tried by a jury, shall be otherwise reexamined in any court of the United States, than according to the rules of the common law."

Black politicians, the Democratic Party, and now a Black jurist did not want a jury to decide on the merits of the case and determine the damages, although these were triable issues of fact, which should be heard by a jury.

As part of our filings we alleged various members of city leadership had engaged in the process of racketeering as defined by the federal racketeering laws. The collusion among governments, elected officials, and private companies to control certain marketplaces was, in our opinion, a classic case of racketeering. For making such an allegation, Judge Marshall fined our company $80,000, calling the allegation preposterous. In 2020, a deputy to a Los Angeles city councilman pled guilty to racketeering charges that had been instituted by the FBI against them. An additional Los Angeles city councilman was arrested and charged with racketeering. Perhaps our allegations were not as preposterous as Judge Marshall would have one believe.

As also mentioned before, this denial to enter the free market and participate in this communications technology sector, as a Black leadership team in the United States, was a crushing double blow. The judge basically gave the city carte blanche to withhold the rights of the majority of Black citizens within its city limits. We cannot and do not feel these rulings are fair when the abuse and effects are so damaging, visible, and egregious.

There is no way for any group of people to determine what is in their best interest if they cannot speak on all media platforms with other members of the group. These communications enhance or influence the activities within their own community. Who should determine what is needed within a community? The concept of freedom gives you the right to determine what your needs are.

The fact that all elected officials have sworn in their oath of office to uphold the law of the United States Constitution means these Black politicians and judges have simply disregarded their oath of office. The Constitution seems only secondary to their personal financial needs and status, which makes for bad leadership under any conditions.

In my opinion, the City of Los Angeles and Tom Bradley used a Black federal judge that was appointed by a Democratic president to deny the rights that were unanimously supported by the United States Supreme Court. In the ten years we were under the jurisdiction of this Black female judge, we never received a jury trial, although numerous trial dates were set and then abandoned. Was this due to the potential damage to Bradley's image and the other Black politicians involved in a trial? Was this process to provide protection to a corrupt political system emanating from the office of Mayor Bradley?

I believe the Democratic Party feared the possible dilution of the Black vote if they allowed Preferred Communications into the media marketplace, as well as the potential for news about the corrupt and racist treatment of South Central to spread to other cities in the United States because of the recognition and standing of Los Angeles as a media hub. Without Black

America, the Democratic Party is no longer competitive in the national political marketplace. Was this their fear?

When we tried to raise the issue of monopolies during our hearings before the US District Court, Judge Marshall refused to allow the issue of violations of the federal antitrust laws to be brought into consideration. The City of Los Angeles created an unregulated monopoly, and then a single federal judge decided that potential competitors cannot discuss an obvious outcome. If you cannot, in a free market, bring up the issue of unregulated monopolies created by governments, then you cannot seek a redress from government for its misuse of its power.

Judge Marshall further ruled that we could not bring up the criminal violations that we had alleged against politicians for many years. She also denied our ability to make an issue of the segregation that had been created during the licensing process. And there it was: judge and jury.

Chapter 5

BETRAYAL LEADS TO A LEADERSHIP VOID

May I remind you, Black America pays the price for a lack of leadership. This lack of leadership is demonstrated by those who claim to be leaders but sell us out every chance they get. When you have large groups of people without leadership, anarchy sometimes arises. Black America is on the brink of anarchy because of our reliance upon the Democratic Party to help us participate within governmental systems. The failure of Black politicians and the Democratic Party are tied together.

Our system in the United States is predicated on people seeking goals. In contrast, a void is simply empty space with nothing in it. When leadership is absent, we have a void. If the void is not filled by people seeking goals within a lawful society that treats everyone as equals, the void will be filled by other means, dramatically impacting the group, which should be led as a whole. If individuals must find their own answers to complex problems, leadership and group cohesion suffer. This is a highly inefficient method of resolving issues that affect entire communities.

The price paid by Black America for failed leadership is evidenced by everything bad in Black America. If it is bad, Black America is almost certainly overrepresented—think of areas such as poverty and poor education. If it is good, Black America gets less than the average American. Failure of leadership to bring Black America forward in society is culpable. Three things you do not want to be in America are broke, incarcerated, and homeless.

Black America has the highest degree of poverty in America. Black America has a higher level of incarceration as a percentage of its population than any other group in America. Black America has the lowest education level of any other group in America, which leads to low wages and greater chances of being unemployed, underemployed, or laid off during economic downturns. These realities indicate a failure of leadership.

The purpose of leadership is to provide tools and opportunities to those who seek to make an improvement in their lives. These tools are often little more than small amounts of education and information to change their status in the employment pool. A leadership void would leave the average citizen with no access to the necessary tools to accomplish a common goal. They could not access those tools because the intermediary, the politician, did not provide assistance or support in any effort— because the politician did not get a personal financial benefit or other favor for his or her support. So efforts by enterprise and industry are slowed.

This void of leadership was partially filled with the expansion of gangs within urban communities. Could this expansion be directly tied to a lack of available media within the community? My partners and I believed more media within the community would give the citizens the ability to better obtain information that could assist community members in making better decisions about crime and drug use.

Historically, gangs competed with parents and schools for the attention of the inner-city youth. The media were a much greater influence than their parents, as indicated earlier, because of the amount of time children spent with television and other electronic media. Just look to see how many inner-city kids are looking at screens in their hands in this day and age.

No locally controlled media were available then or are available now to combat the issues of local communities. Many of the issues of 1980 remain issues today and were voiced in our 1980 applications to the city, along with some innovative solutions that could have been provided by cable television and the new technology at that time.

Gangs are developed by the economic functions within America. Gangs work on the supply and demand curve for illegal drugs or legal drugs, as the case may be—a shadow economy to fill the space for which there is no other alternative in the community. The substantial demand for drugs within the United States led to an illegal organizational venture to provide such drugs regardless of the law. This attitude has been developed by watching legitimate capitalism fail to enter poor communities within the United States.

During Prohibition in the 1920s and 1930s, gangs were developed by the disenfranchised in order to take advantage of the demand for alcohol. Much of the public wanted to consume alcohol but were denied because of the government's prohibition of it as a mood-altering substance and an attempt to reduce crime and enhance health. The public's demand overrode the government's attempt to limit the use of alcohol within society. The criminalization of drugs provided the same stimulus for gangs to develop in order to provide substances that were demanded by millions of Americans. The gangs were once again developed primarily by the disenfranchised.

Leadership is supposed to identify issues that become problems for the community. The failure of leadership means the community is without guidance unless there is some sort of action to preclude the events occurring in this leadership void. Without access to media and without access to leadership, the Black community has been left to fend for itself.

Gangs deal with violations of their code of ethics in a method that is not dissimilar to the government. They use draconian measures to ensure compliance with their demands. While the government may incarcerate you for twenty-five years for drug, firearm, or gang activities, the community also has to contend with the justice of the gangs, which involves simply killing people. Innocent bystanders of all ages are collateral damage. Inhumanity reigns.

South Central became a breeding ground for gangs. The lack of capital investment allowed within the community meant there could be no job creation. Without the creation of jobs, the expansion of crime and gangs would reach epidemic proportions—and was inevitable. Joining a gang was the best-paying job, if you didn't get caught or killed. The lack of information and capital investment within the community would doom the community. The LA city government's answer was simply adding more police forces to the war on drugs and war on gangs. The City of Los Angeles was partially responsible

100

for allowing gang development in South Central. Their efforts were too little, too late.

The gangs provided a sense of belonging to Black youth who felt disenfranchised, along with the rest of Black America. Since there was no leadership to help instruct the young people, they had no ability to make decisions based upon rational information available to them. As there was no information provided to them about the effects of joining gangs and participating in criminal behavior at such a young age, oftentimes between eleven and fourteen, the ability of gangs to recruit was pervasive. Being an ex-con was lauded in the neighborhood, as the person had survived the system.

Participation in gangs gave some young people a sense of security they did not have walking the streets and dodging bullets in their own community. Members of the South Central community did not expect the police to provide protection because they were looked upon as an occupation force. The gangs controlled South Central—not the police or a bunch of politicians. There's a lingering distrust of authority in Black America today. Considering the treatment that is captured on the videos being publicized around the country today, imagine what was going on before we had that technology.

As gangs were expanding during the 1980s, the City of Los Angeles was limiting the rights of the residents of South Central to communicate among themselves. Cable television could have assisted in allowing citizens to look at and alleviate problems existing within their own community. Since the government, with and in the form of politicians, chose to ignore the problems within the community, the community had the right to speak and find solutions for these troubling issues. Being able to speak in your own community about issues affecting it is called freedom of the press or, in the twenty-first century, freedom of the media.

The key element was a lack of leadership, which created a vacuum of guidance within the community. Black America was under attack during the drug wars, and there was no leadership to assist them in dealing with the issues. These issues included not only the drugs that existed within the community but the level of force that was being used on a continual basis within the community and against the community's children.

Gangs are the ultimate example of civil disobedience. Gangs are able to create their own rules and regulations. They are also able to enforce such rules and regulations with violence. The ability to ignore civil law and create gang law permeated the South Central community.

By deeming the police a force of occupation, a degree of legitimacy was granted to the gangs by the community. The militarization of the police force served to create fear of the police within the community. The use of tanks and aircraft as part of the police presence made them a military presence, as opposed to a civilian police presence. Police abuse of young Black men served to assist and popularize gangs. Remember a few paragraphs ago when I said ex-cons were lauded? Young Black men in urban areas were caught between gangs and police, and both were deadly to them.

Lawmakers, including Black lawmakers, expect blind allegiance by the citizens to the laws they create and pass. It is also the responsibility of those same elected officials and community leaders to provide information allowing their citizens to understand the purpose and nature of the laws being passed. Without attempts by lawmakers to help their constituents understand those laws before and after they are passed into law, the disenfranchised can be reluctant to embrace the laws made by those who won't listen to their complaints. The respect for the order of law is also diminished when those who create the law do not abide by it. This is what the rest of America sees, Black America included.

The federal government continued its attempts to salvage a drug war that had already been lost many years earlier. In order to lend some degree of legitimacy to the continuing war, in 1994 and thereafter it was necessary to incarcerate large numbers of people to show the American public the government was hard at work protecting the country at the federal, state, and local levels. Large numbers of these incarcerated people turned out to be minorities, primarily because they didn't have the resources to defend themselves against the unlimited resources of the government. The leadership in Black America did not consider alternatives to incarceration as treatment for the drug problem. But we know the drug problem cannot be jailed out of existence. Could Black media have helped?

I cannot say that any one solution is the best solution, but I think all solutions need to be reviewed in light of the circumstances in which we find ourselves. This deadly war and the mass incarceration of minority citizens are extremely expensive, divisive, and don't provide the protection of society the government claims. Tens of thousands of people, in all parts of America, are dying each year from opioid and prescription medication overdoses on top of cocaine and heroin addiction, but we talk about the inner city. Perhaps some level of treatment could save some of the lives being lost or incarcerated. The criminalization of drug addiction does not benefit the individual or society.

The drug wars have done little but create an obscene profit base for those who are willing to take advantage of the economics of illegal drugs, with ruined lives, gang deaths, and dangerous inner-city neighborhoods at the hands of the gangs and the addicted. Decriminalization would take the profit out of drugs, provide treatment for those who sought it, and lead to a reduction of the gang violence permeated by protecting "turf" in the drug world. The decriminalization of drugs would serve as a dramatic benefit in minority communities with tens of thousands of young men being rounded up and incarcerated for nonviolent crimes and being denied public assistance because of their past crimes. No one in the Democratic Party, except the mayor of Baltimore in 1988, has been willing to stand up for the decriminalization of drugs, despite the fact that their communities could benefit from such legislation. Is there another viable idea out there?

There should also be an expectation of justice, even if you don't have money for a lawyer. Being at the hands of the system without money would be laughable if it wasn't so sad. Elected officials are supposed be your protection to ensure justice from the government. Citizens are often arrested based upon nothing more than a police officer's statement that he may have smelled pot in a car. Once a person is in custody, the criminal justice system grinds up low-income individuals who do not have the ability or education to assist in their own defense.

My group watched the City of Los Angeles spend millions of dollars against our cable television case, which only served to show that even with money you cannot expect justice in a corrupt political and judicial environment. These incarcerated lives are more Black capital being wasted, dealing with government jurisprudence as opposed to spending money creating jobs within the community.

Citizens who could not afford even minimal bail were often forced to remain in jail for many times longer than they would have been sentenced to for the crime for which they were charged. This bail fiasco caused many people who were innocent to confess to crimes they did not commit. We also need to touch on the horrific treatment within the jail system and prison system. People were often held for months, and even years, without a trial, with no ability to bail themselves out of jail after the charges had been filed. This is a form of government injustice and people not having a right to seek release from these conditions is destroying inner-city communities. Once again, leadership within the Black community has turned a deaf ear to the suffering of young citizens caught up in the cross fire of the drug war.

Living in a war zone of normal citizens, gangs, and the police with a continuous threat of violence has created mental disorders in a number of young people. They suffer the same effects of PTSD as soldiers involved in war on foreign land, but without the resources for treatment. With no medical coverage or resources, it was not possible to have their mental illness treated at an early stage, to avoid the need for intervening legal implications. The conversion of a medical situation into a criminal justice situation is simply an atrocity upon the human beings who suffer from mental illness.

It is estimated that at least 20 percent of the prison population has some form of mental illness. The largest mental health facility in the United States is based on Rikers Island, a New York City jail and prison. Once again, failures of leadership allow situations like these to occur.

Let's talk about another problem in the inner city. The numbers racket, run by organized crime in the early- to the mid-twentieth century, was taken over by state governments. This form of gambling and frittering away of money with astronomical odds against ever winning started in the 1980s, when states began to offer the lottery. In 1983, the State of California authorized the institution of a lottery system, saying profits would be used to increase education funds for the children of the state. The lottery was voted on as a proposition by the general public in 1983. An organized crime that had existed since the 1920s in the United States was now to become another government-protected monopoly.

The same Black politicians who had spoken so vociferously against the numbers racket within the community were now proponents of the lottery system. Now that it had been taken over by the government, there was no criminal behavior involved. But what they didn't know, or didn't care to know, was that the lottery would have a much more substantial impact in low-income communities than in other communities. This was due to the amount of disposable income being applied toward lottery games. Low-income people have less money to spend overall, so they were spending money they couldn't afford to spend. Do I buy a lottery ticket or save it to buy food? Pay my utility bills? Pay my rent?

Being involved in the numbers racket prior to the installation of a lottery would subject a person to substantial prison time. It was long considered a crime to prey upon the poor. The numbers racket was even more honest under organized crime because they paid better results, and often the numbers were tied to horses who were running in races in that area. The lottery is nothing of the sort. It is merely a numerical system designed to take hundreds of billions of dollars out of the system and put it into the hands of the government and friends of politicians.

The creation of the lottery in California is a classic example of what happens when those who are affected by government creations do not have a right to petition the government nor to have their views heard in a reasonable fashion. The inner-city community lacked both leadership and the ability to communicate within its own boundaries. This is not to say that the lottery would not have passed anyway—people always seem eager to gamble. But has the California education system been enhanced like the original proposition indicated?

Now the State of California is engaged in licensing and protecting the business of selling and cultivating marijuana. But there are people still serving life sentences for the sale and cultivation of marijuana. The crime was previously deemed so offensive by the government that they locked a person up for a life sentence for engaging in it prior to legalization. The government has seemingly changed its attitude toward marijuana, now considering it an acceptable substance to be used within society. There are marijuana stores in LA like there are liquor stores in New York. Marijuana is not legal in New York.

If the substance is now legal, could it have been so dangerous previously as to warrant the unlimited detention of citizens imprisoned for its use or cultivation? We must carefully reexamine those previous sentences with the intent of having prisoners released from custody if their only crime was related to marijuana. So now we have a merry-go-round of the government taking over industries (gambling and marijuana) that previously represented criminal behavior, with the stigma of criminal behavior removed. The same industries became socially acceptable when the government started doing things instead of individuals or nongovernmental entities. But people are still in jail based on former laws. It is socially acceptable now that the government has taken over, and the government controls the media, which does not dispute the government.

Government claims its interest in drugs is to protect the health and welfare of the citizens of the country. How can anyone believe this when in fact tobacco kills more than a quarter of a million people each year in the United States and tobacco companies can still advertise on billboards and magazines and newspapers, including publications that are widely read by youth. Tobacco is a drug according to the FDA. You see plenty of children smoking despite the fact that they are underage. Why is that law so loosely enforced?

The use of alcohol within our society has killed millions of people. Drinking and driving has had a significant impact upon our society. The violation of these laws does not lead to life imprisonment, despite the fact that people are often killed by drunk drivers. Alcohol is a drug according to the FDA. Underage drinking is common in most states. Underage drinking is an epidemic at colleges and universities throughout the United States. Where is law enforcement on college campuses? Underage drinking runs rampant and is not policed.

When you have a leadership void, you have no voice in how

various laws are enforced. Certain drugs can be used by children without any repercussions. Use of other drugs is subject to the maximum penalties, especially when the user is a minority person. I have used all these examples to ask if this is really justice or if these arbitrary laws are used only to incarcerate minority people.

Chapter 6

IT'S ALL ABOUT MONEY

I challenge anyone to name one thing not affected by money in the United States, be it religion, education, politics, or riding a bicycle. The fact that money is so intertwined with the daily life of all Americans, and many citizens of other countries as well, means we should give decisions regarding its utilization great consideration.

There is an entire field of study about money known as economics. It is taught at all major universities from the undergraduate level to the doctorate level because of its importance to the financial health of our society.

One definition describes economics as "the branch of knowledge concerned with the production, consumption, and transfer of wealth." Another definition of economics is "the process of attempting to meet unlimited wants and desires by society with limited resources." Labor and work are forms of capital as they are exchanged for money, which is in turn used for spending power as part of the economy.

There are many names for money. It is called cash, capital, rent, groceries, and medicine. There are also numerous slang terms for money because money affects everyone. Every society, past and present, has had a form of money or barter equivalent—this for that. Money is a medium of exchange, and without something to exchange it for, money is merely paper, metal, or a number for a swipe. The term *capital* is the one I will focus on because it refers to the investment of money for the production of goods and services within our society.

Do you think of money when you consider what America is about? Economics is necessary to understand the framework of America or any nation doing business within or outside its borders. America is structured and defined as a capitalist democracy. The ability to participate in a capitalist democracy without capital is substantially limited. Capital is the root word of *capitalist* and *capitalism*.

But consider: when local, state, or national governments keep you from participating in the free enterprise system of capitalism, they are keeping you from participating in the American economic system. The capitalist democracy determines the relationship between economics and poverty—those who have money and those who do not. We expect our leaders to help us participate or gain participation within the overall economic system and thereby become part of the capitalist system.

Poverty and being low-income are economic conditions. They are the lowest capital classifications, indicating they have less money than other groups, which is a problem in our society if they cannot get basic resources for their everyday lives and gain economic traction to better their situation.

So what's the solution? We must first develop an understanding of the basic concepts of economics and how they affect everyday life.

In low-income situations, information is restricted or not available to the people who need it most. First Amendment privileges are stymied, and capitalism is no longer a welcoming, independent free market activity. If government systems foster conditions that prohibit you from engaging in the free market system, you are being deprived of participating in American society overall.

"Low-income" classification has many implications. Among these implications are crime, poor medical outcomes, and negative legal outcomes. Lower availability of financial resources means lower availability of the resources democracy provides and a lower ability to fight legal charges that are the basis of the American justice system.

I will not go into a long dissertation to support this position, but I have great confidence that most Americans believe this to be true—whether we like it or not. Most of us accept that the rich and those with substantial political influence receive different treatment under the law than the middle class and those without money.

If you do not understand the basic economics governing the American financial system, you cannot understand how America works. You may think of economics as some complex theory, but in fact it is rather simple. It is subject to the "other" golden rule, "He who has the gold, makes the rules." Here's another axiom: "You cannot have so much money that you can't go broke. You can have so little money that you can't get away from being broke."

In Texas, a young man from a wealthy family got drunk and killed four people with his car in a crosswalk. After being convicted of vehicular manslaughter, the judge said the man was too affluent to understand the ramifications of his actions and therefore should not be sentenced to jail time. This became known as "affluenza," or the disease of getting off from legal charges because you are wealthy.

This same treatment doesn't apply to those with limited incomes and a lack of education. It would seem more applicable to those who do not have the resources to understand the consequences of their behavior, rather than severely punishing them for any legal problem.

In New York, a man was killed by the police for selling single cigarettes on the street, according to the police. Death for cigarettes is justice displaced in a somewhat random fashion. It does not take a rocket scientist to figure out the color of the skin of the drunk driver who went free and the cigarette seller who was killed by the police. They are examples of the extremes.

So money and justice are closely tied. Those defendants without money are substantially more likely to be convicted and incarcerated than defendants who have private attorneys. The difference between public defenders and private attorneys is money.

Public defenders - those who work for the state to defend clients who have no money for private attorneys - cannot effectively compete with a district attorney or attorney general because of their workload and limited resources. The egregious difference in the amount spent by the prosecution as opposed to the amount spent for defense represents the inequality of the financial resources.

The district attorney generally has little regard for guilt or innocence because they are evaluated and rewarded based on conviction rates. Like in most other industries, people will push the envelope a little bit in order to enhance their own personal rewards. The risk/reward envelope in the inner city is fraught with the legal penalties from the drug war and anti-crime bills that can mean long prison terms for the disenfranchised. The destruction of thousands of lives is secondary to these unjust sentences, as seen by the people in those inner-city neighborhoods.

Economics affects outcomes. Your chances of participating in the systems necessary to prosper and improve your condition within society are diminished without capital. There are exceptions, but I think I am safe to say that in order to fully participate in the American system you must be a participant. The inability to fully participate in the economic system, which is a basis of any capitalistic country, keeps people from obtaining the benefits of economic development.

Jobs are the primary interface of the citizen with the overall economy. Education is one of the benefits that goes with economic development. The higher your level of education, the higher your ability to participate in the economic system and to get benefits from it. The better the education, the higher the income.

Economic status is determined not only by how much money you make but how you spend that money. Poverty is all about money or the lack thereof. You cannot spend more than you make and also have money to invest. Without money to invest, your community cannot create jobs and infrastructure necessary for the growth and development of your community.

115

So, now, if you are able to have money, what do you do with it? It's a decision of how much to spend and how much to save. How do you spend your money? Do you invest with the expectation you shall receive an increased return? Will you spend it on consumer goods that depreciate as soon as you get them out the merchants' door or as soon as they can send them to you? We all want money and we all need money.

Most of the advertising you see on television, your internet service, or your social media site is designed to stimulate your mind to spend money to the benefit of the sponsor of that advertisement. Advertising is a form of pleasure and consumer-driven brainwashing. You know they are trying to influence your mind.

One of the most important issues in the economic order is supply and demand. Think of toilet paper. When supply exceeds demand, prices will go down. Conversely, when demand exceeds supply, prices will go up. By creating artificial demand, companies keep prices high for products and services that could be less expensive and therefore more affordable.

Some people would rather give the appearance of having money with all their worldly possessions than actually have money from investing. You provide the goods and services you cherish for your ego rather than for their usefulness. The stores, trends, and advertising tell you that you need it now. They make these objects easy to get with exorbitant interest rates. They pull you into the interest trap. Then you get stuck paying two to three times the interest rates of higher economic categories because of your economic status, so your dollars buy less.
There are plenty of people in America to tell you where you are in terms of status, but few to tell you how you got there.

As Gil Scott-Heron said, "America leads the world in shocks. Unfortunately, America does not lead the world in deciphering the cause of shock." Think of getting your credit card bills. Did you really charge that much this month?

Money is power. If you can keep it, get a better job, or get better interest rates, and you've got more money and chances to get loans and increase your capital.

Capital is necessary to create and grow businesses within any community. You can't spend your way out of poverty.

On a business level, this means you have to be able to save money and/or get financial resources of some kind. Capital creates jobs and fulfills wants and needs within the society. The growth and development of such businesses allow for jobs and stability within the community. Capital is power both on a political and business level. Capital is the supreme power on a political scale. The ability to raise funds to support the advertising and distribution of information relative to a candidate is funded by contributors, including those who will benefit from the candidate being in office.

It is especially necessary for those who are at the lower end of the economic spectrum to have more respect for money because of the influence it can have upon their lives—an attitude of saving for better credit ratings, for example, to lift themselves from poverty. But low-income people are juggling scant monetary resources to fight to provide basic necessities for themselves and their families.

Their money provides the necessities for their family to exist. It provides housing, food, and clothing. Without being able to create business opportunities or to fund education beyond a high school degree, the people within your own community frequently cannot transition from poverty to a more desirable level of living.

Economic forces vary in a country as wide and diverse as the United States. Sometimes, even the government cannot control many of the economic forces that affect the general public. Think of a natural disaster like a flood or hurricane. Yet citizens, both individually and collectively, can dramatically influence the economic order within a community. If there is an economic problem, there is an economic solution. When the flow of money goes to those who already have the most money in society and circumvents low-income communities, poverty cannot be eradicated or reduced.

You're free to spend your money any way you choose, but don't spend it and complain about the results after you have consumed the goods you purchased. You can make money and spend it, or you can make money by saving money and investing what you saved. How you utilize your money is an important factor in determining what your benefits will be from your money. Do you seek only consumer benefits of entertainment and spending everything, or do you seek long-term benefits of investment and return on investment? The smart answer is to decide to save.

If you are merely a consumer in the economic order, and not a producer, you are destined to never fully benefit from the economic system of America. You stay on the same level as your salary. The inability of Black America to fully participate in the production side of goods and services they consume blocks participation and growth within the overall society. If

118

you are a producer or owner, your income capacity increases dramatically. But even if you understand economics and the opportunities you should take advantage of, you will be blocked by politicians seeking benefits and bribes from your ideas and work.

Another weapon used against low-income neighborhoods is the payday loan. Such loans give a person a false impression that they have more money, for a time, but tie them to interest rates in excess of 200 percent in a year. California used to have usury laws that prohibited the lending of money at a rate in excess of 10 percent. Payday loan companies are able to offer these loans because the government has given them authority to become the legal equivalent of loan sharks. Do you think perhaps the same politicians who gave them this authority receive a percentage of that money as political contributions? Rather than being at the mercy of payday loans, the deferral of purchases can lead to a better utilization of limited financial resources.

If the leaders of your community, city, and state are not improving your economic situation or have no interest in promoting free enterprise beyond their benefits and bribes, they are fundamentally worthless.

Historically, the ability to interface with the economy has been determined substantially by the leadership you have chosen. It is abundantly apparent in court cases and other cases that politicians are not securing our protection under the Constitution. In a capitalist society, those who don't provide capital and community improvements are basically worthless from an economic standpoint. Failed leadership provides neither. The inability of Black America to fully participate in the capital side of the economic order in America must be partially laid at the feet of the Black leadership that is supposed be providing guidance toward a better future in minority neighborhoods. This has not happened. Instead, a group of people who I believe see themselves as "Black political royalty" established themselves as greedy middlemen for all participation within what should be free enterprise—as opposed to a controlled enterprise with them as the bottleneck. They have the power to say, "I will let you do *this* in my district, but not *that*."

The politicians have created economic embargo zones in their districts with their greed, inadvertently or not, which damage the people within those zones. An economic embargo increases the price of goods and services within a community. It also limits jobs within the community because the lack of capital investment available within the community makes it harder for citizens to gain skills, capital, and education. The right of self-determination is destroyed. Then capital from minority communities is exported, and no community can prosper or survive without capital.

The government, via politicians, created and enforced an economic embargo against inner-city communities. These communities were not allowed to invest in themselves or have the new technology, as in our case, that could have changed the lives of so many in America through jobs, reinvestment, and information.

Acquiring new technologies, as cable television was at the time, and attracting substantial industry are the keys for low-income neighborhoods to grow with America into more stable and prosperous economies. But who will invest when Black politicians are doing nothing to battle crime and instability in those neighborhoods?

The inability of local communities to get business and thus reinvest some of the profits and funds developed by technology and industry hampers their growth and will continue to do so in coming years. The economic damage is not always felt immediately, but it is certainly felt over longer periods of time. The economic damage caused by not having industry and technology investing in inner cities could impact minority communities forever.

The politicians' meddling in the free market system continues to limit the potential of low-income and minority participants. This interference, brought about by uncaring and unprincipled leadership, includes bribes and selling protection to other businesses that might be competitive with your local one. So you're not allowed to enter the marketplace.

Entire industries have been blocked out for the benefit of rich friends of politicians, especially minority and inner-city areas. For our cable business, it was Mr. Broad who got the license, didn't use the license for years, and then sold it. He was able to sell the exclusive right to control the new technology in South Central.

This travesty has been perpetrated by Black politicians who are too busy selling out the community to take the time to find out the effect of that sellout. In the cable television industry alone the government prohibited the $50 million investment and thousands of jobs outlined in our proposal from being created in South Central Los Angeles in 1980. The community was left with no cable television and the

121

lost potential of those jobs and $50 million investment for almost ten years.

Black political leaders seem ignorant of their negative efforts in the community but consistently try to tell you how to run your business. They limit your ability to use your own assets to develop needed products and services that would benefit your community. They try to pass laws requiring you to go to their offices and to their friends in order to conduct business within your own community. We went to dozens of offices! This is part of a power play to penalize those who do not support their subversive behavior.

The ability to effectively utilize your money is one of the things that separates the various economic strata within American society. Emphasis on effective. Clearly there is a section of society that has always had money, because money has always existed. There have been rich people in the United States for generations and centuries. This is one of the aspects that draws people from all over the world to the United States: the ability to become wealthy and live in a place where there is peace and protection for them, their families, and their assets.

There will always be those at the bottom and those at the top. Those at the top generally have some political affiliation or backing that allows them to remain at the top. The thing that has made America great is the middle class and the ability to transition from the bottom to the top. There are thousands of Black millionaires and a substantial number of Black billionaires, so it is possible. Getting there by using and understanding capital is the key.

The lack of capital is a major reason employment cannot be created within certain communities. Investment and then partial reinvestment from within the community generates jobs and economic security. This goes for the country as a whole and Black communities specifically. Lack of capital has had dire consequences in South Central Los Angeles over the past four decades. Once again, South Central is only one example of what goes on in urban minority communities throughout the United States.

For example, our "stolen" cable opportunity could have provided net positive cash flow of funds for the South Central community. The cable television service industry around the United States has been in the hundreds of billions of dollars over the last thirty-five years. What would have been the effect of a partial reinvestment of this money within the community it serves? Think of local tax revenue, job creation, and donations into the community.

No community or group can allow capital to continually leave the community without it being replaced. Without capital, no community can participate fully in the capitalist system that is the basis of the American economy.

Capital is the substance the turns ideas into reality. In business terms, there's nothing that does not require the use of capital to make it a reality.

No economic entity can continue to exist when there are more expenses than income. This goes for individuals, corporations, and governments. Governments, however, have an advantage because of their abilities to tax citizens and print money. Even the ability to tax is no guarantee, as several cities have filed for bankruptcy protection or gone bankrupt over the last forty years. Since 2010, almost seventy municipalities have filed for bankruptcy protection.

So how do businesses stay in business? You must be profitable. The decision of how much profit to seek on your legitimate business or personal investment is up to the individual and not controlled by government in most cases. You must make a profit in order to continue in business or make money on your investment. If you do not intend to make a profit, you should consider becoming a nonprofit organization with some public benefit. Merely losing money is not a public benefit.

I, a Black citizen, was raised when there was a thriving middle class in America. I, and others, believe this is what made America a great nation. The ability to ascend to higher economic status within America, within a generation, with hard work and capital, is what separates America from many other nations. Some of those coming to America bring financial capital with them or can get investment capital for their businesses from home.

A couple of years after I finished college, my father asked me a question. My father had only a high school education, but he had good commonsense. He said, semi-facetiously, "You're a bright guy. You finished college and you got a job with a major international financial firm—maybe you can answer my question." His question was, "Why would a man spend $300 million to get a job that pays $250,000?" He was actually perplexed by the idea of so much money being spent by a presidential candidate. As he shook his head and walked away, he simply stated, "That can't be honest." The salary has not appreciably changed, but the amount spent to get it has risen almost exponentially. Yes, why?

In my work and my efforts to get a cable television license, I have seen firsthand how money and politics go hand in hand to decide who will rule any community. In poverty-stricken communities the money cannot come from the citizens, therefore it comes from the political party that controls these communities. In Black America, it is the Democratic Party who decides which people become their candidates and provides the money necessary to elect those candidates, who then become politicians. The election of these politicians is not for the benefit of the citizens but rather for the benefit of the Democratic Party.

Why do they spend all that money, as my father asked? They spend it to gain power and convince you, the voter, of their superior candidates. "Convincing" in this day and age happens through political advertising, mostly via electronic media.

The purpose is to push particular candidates' issues into the forefront of your mind and to convince you that the candidate shares your views or is better than the other candidate. The one with the most money and advertising generally wins. The candidates can say anything they choose without any consideration for truth, the reasonableness of their ideas, or their real ability to fulfill the promises.

One reason why politicians get so much advertising money is that their coffers are filled by the people they, and the Democratic Party, actually work for—the large contributors. Flashy ads that change with the polling can make the candidate more attractive, as long as you have the money to pay for the advertising. What candidates say in the advertising, more often than not, has more to do with polling than any other factor and does not indicate what they will actually do once they are in office.

If you want some idea of what they're going to do in office, simply look at the largest contributors to any individual candidate, and you'll see what they're going to be working on. Their government paycheck might be small in comparison to private business salaries. It's illegal to get direct payments from contributors for the work they do on their behalf, but there are numerous ways to funnel money to politicians. Free trips and employing relatives are just a couple of ways to "enrich" a politician. Campaign contributions are used to control elected officials, promote their reelection, and maintain their position once they're in place.

Money, media, and politicians go hand in hand. The money buys the media, which is necessary for the politicians to maintain their place in office. The media are necessary in order to continually reinforce the supposed positions of the politicians. Whether the stated positions are true or false is fundamentally irrelevant. The media do very little to verify the statements made by politicians as long as they pay for the advertising.

Let's look at an example of money in politics in action in an inner-city neighborhood. Inglewood, a predominantly minority city, is a classic example of what can be accomplished when large sums of money are put on the table. The investors who wanted to build a new 80,000-seat stadium in Inglewood were able to get all the permits and approvals they needed within four months after they identified the project. This simply required various state legislators and the City of Inglewood to eliminate some of the requirements other citizens are subject to in the permit and approvals process. This seems a bit strange because in Inglewood it sometimes takes up to a year to get a permit to put a garage behind your own house.

In contrast, consider not getting approval to build a four-unit apartment building, on land you already own, zoned for that type of building. It generally takes up to a year to get the approvals necessary to build housing for the citizens of the Inglewood community. Inglewood is just another small city in which, in the case of a huge stadium versus a private citizen, the citizen is subject to lesser service by the city. The mayor of Inglewood and a substantial part of the city council are Black. How does this new stadium enhance the local Black community? In the short run, and very pertinent to the residents of the area, it increases the rent and decreases the availability of housing for those who have been living in this community for the last twenty-five years. It also destroys small independent Black business, and no plans were made for alternate housing for those who were inconvenienced or displaced.

Local Inglewood residents were subject to requirements, including environmental impact studies, on their projects. But when the stadium people came to town, did they have to do an impact study to determine the effect of bringing tens of thousands of cars into the area, with no new streets? All the liberal dogma about environmental studies and reports and concerns were simply overlooked when the big money came to town. The California legislature, which was controlled by the Democratic Party, simply waived the need to comply with any environmental impact reports or studies.

Television programming, especially news programming, plays a large role in how people find out what's happening in their community. A substantial part of the news programming cycle—or any network programming, for that matter—is the advertising segments that go into the news program. You will rarely see anything on a news station that reflects negatively upon one of their advertisers because they are paid by the advertisers and do not want to do anything to jeopardize their ad revenue. Things got so bad that now broadcast companies have to identify if their company is involved in any product they are putting on their programs—like books or movies from their conglomerate company.

Most news programs have degenerated into little more than random pieces of useless information or gossip, with some tragedy mixed in, to fill time until the next advertisement— their revenue generator. Approximately one-third of the time of news programming is paid advertising. Advertising allows the payer of funds to express their point of view and give you information about whatever they are selling or offering.

How much screen time is actually given to advertising as opposed to news on a news program? As a test, I selected one news program, the *NBC Nightly News*, and calculated the amount of advertising shown in one half-hour news program. I'm quite sure the other national news programs have very similar advertising percentages to the program I selected. The program had nine minutes of advertising in a thirty minute program, excluding promotional features for their own network shows. So if you watch the program in real time, without fast-forwarding, approximately 30 percent of the time watching "news" is spent looking at the advertisements of their sponsors.

A stated purpose of news programming is to attract customers to the advertisers. The advertisers expect that if you have faith in the news programming, you will have faith in what is advertised as well.

In the earlier years of television, news was considered a public service to the community, often less profit-oriented than entertainment television, and was broadcast as such. This has changed today. News has morphed into entertainment to justify the expense of awarding licenses to companies otherwise engaged in the business of entertainment, like Disney and Viacom. Accordingly, the news division is now considered a profit center rather than a service to the general public, whose public airways they use for their own personal profit—public airways instituted and paid for by the taxpayers of this nation.

The ability of advertising to alter the public perception of a specific event or company is clearly demonstrated in the fraud recently committed by Wells Fargo Bank. The purpose of advertising is to encourage you to buy a product, adjust your perception of a product, or reinforce your perception about a product or a specific institution—in this case, a bank. Wells Fargo opened more than three million fraudulent accounts in the names of people who didn't apply for or want such accounts. The behavior of Wells Fargo Bank is the definition of fraud.

When the fraud was discovered by government authorities, the bank received a fine, but no one was placed in jail for this multimillion-dollar fraud that would have placed a regular citizen in jail. This widespread fraud must have included thousands of the bank's employees. No single employee can open millions of new accounts. To me, the use of thousands of people to perpetrate massive fraud is the fundamental definition of organized crime. Again, different sets of laws for individuals or companies to make their frauds go away. While they may pay money to resolve the criminal behavior, they will not be forced to undergo criminal penalties. You have a different perspective of robbing and stealing from people when you don't have to face the prospect of going to prison. More examples of this differing treatment can be seen in the punishments of those in the inner city versus those living elsewhere.

While the news may have covered this issue several times over a three-month period as government proceedings against Wells Fargo started, there was no coverage of this issue over the subsequent year. But Wells Fargo's advertising indicates what a great bank they are and their concern for the average consumer. Their capital allows them to reprogram the public's mind about the behavior of Wells Fargo so that they are viewed as a community resource as opposed to a bank involved in fraudulent activities. Fraud is forgotten by many as Wells Fargo refines its image of integrity through the media and advertising. No one was convicted of their criminal charges because they were able to pay money to avoid such treatment in the criminal justice system, unlike citizens of the inner city. File a single fraudulent loan application and you will probably end up in jail.

The repetition of Wells Fargo Bank ads versus the news media coverage of the massive fraud that had been perpetrated by Wells Fargo is an example of what happens when major corporations simply disregard the law and then use advertising in the public media in order to reinforce an artificial trust. They are subject to monetary fines for their fraudulent behavior, but the average citizen is subject to prison sentences for the same fraudulent behavior. The difference is that the one who is subject to the monetary fine perpetrates that behavior on a much wider basis than the individual who receives a prison sentence. How much money did they make by breaking the law? How much money did they pay when they were caught?

Wells Fargo's ability to pay to repeat the image they developed as opposed to the image of their fraudulence in a court of law is based upon the amount of capital, advertising capital, they have to spend. Wells Fargo is continually telling you how wonderfully they treat their customers. If you tell someone something enough times, most will believe it, despite the facts. P. T. Barnum was right: if we look at advertising, companies are trying to make us suckers every day.

Another example of creating a false advertising image is BP's involvement in the oil and gas disaster and tragedy that occurred off the Louisiana Gulf Coast in 2010. BP was able to neutralize any negative comments made on the news by utilizing advertising that described the great things they were doing for society and for endangered animals after the damage was done. They did not have to mention that the animals they were trying to protect had been endangered by BP's behavior.

We must bear the responsibility of understanding the media and advertising and how they treat us. We need to understand the power and influence of media on ourselves and our families, especially children, who are so easily influenced by the next fad and strive to fit into their peer group. That is why you see children throwing tantrums in supermarkets for a product with a specific character or name on it. Do not blame the child, but take some blame yourself for allowing your child to be influenced by whatever media they have been consuming.

Advertisements tell you that you need something now. They make it easy for you to get it with exorbitant interest rates that double the price of that item over a one- or two-year time frame. This is a standard approach that increases the likelihood that poor people will stay poor by overpaying for things that they do not need immediately but are goaded into obtaining by continuous advertising. Your mind can become conditioned to the message being repeatedly delivered by any advertiser. They make you feel out of touch or abnormal for not having the product they are advertising. Ever see a child in the inner city with $300 sneakers emblazoned with his favorite sports star? Don't think theft—think of parents going without other essentials so the child can fit in with their peer group because advertising told those children they needed those shoes. Think of what that $300 could have gone toward, in products or services or savings for the rest of the family.

So major media advertising makes you think your wants are really your needs. If someone other than yourself can determine what it is that you need, as opposed to want, then they are in control of your life, your opinions, and your actions, and you are destined to remain short of money.

It is about our choices. We must have goals so the choices we make serve to fulfill those goals. Without goals, the effects of your choices are scattershot, all over the place. The purpose of leadership is to identify goals and to assist in reaching them. Goals for large numbers of people need leadership because each individual cannot have broad goals and expect to meet them alone. When leaders fail to fulfill their responsibilities to assist the community in reaching even minimal goals, they are not only failures, but cheats.

The existing housing shortage in Los Angeles and throughout California is fundamentally caused by politicians who make it difficult for independent businesspeople to build new housing. Unless the politician is paid through contributions or some other economic benefit, they will become an impediment to the development. There is no shortage of land and there is no shortage of capital to construct new housing.

The problem is getting government approval, which goes through those politicians, prior to building housing. Once politicians enter a free marketplace, it is no longer free, which leaves urban and minority communities with limited affordable housing. Limited housing causes the price of housing to increase at a higher rate than the incomes of the people who occupy the housing. Down an economic step, homelessness is primarily an economic condition exacerbated by this lack of political integrity.

The free enterprise system should be the very basis of the American economy. Bureaucrats and politicians interfering with free enterprise to their benefit and not their community's benefit is deadly. The inability to enter the free market system limits Black America, further preventing individuals from determining their own economic fortune.

It seems Black leaders want people to seek government assistance instead of providing the necessary tools to participate in the economic system and obtain the funds to live independently through other methods. People come to America from around the world and become successful. Why not people from our own inner cities? With Black politicians locking Black communities out of economic operations within the United States, it's clear that poverty was meant to stay in place. With poverty comes all the negative economic and social effects and their constituents clamoring for more welfare benefits, with no other alternatives. So Black politicians plead for welfare on one hand, destroying opportunities for their constituents to provide for themselves on the other.

The City of Los Angeles simply said to hell with competition as long as its friends are compensated by any new industry within its political ability to regulate. The fact that this method of regulation was both unconstitutional and illegal had no bearing upon those at City Hall. Let's not deceive ourselves: the government and the politicians knew the consequences of unregulated monopolies.

One of the most effective methods of purchasing any product is by comparison shopping. This can be done at the individual level in the same way it is at the corporate level when they are spending millions of dollars for a product or service. Corporate purchases often involve obtaining specific pricing for the product they are seeking from numerous sources. It is important for the individual to understand this concept and to utilize the same concept as they decide how to spend their own money.

Depending upon the government to resolve the same problems that have existed for more than 150 years is not the best situation. If they had any real intention of resolving these issues, or the ability, they would've resolved them by now. The solutions are not as simple as politicians would have you believe because we are dealing with money and with power, and the combination of the two can be good or bad depending on which side of the fence you're on.

Legitimate attempts to enter new businesses, as may be required specifically by your own community, are not supported by Black politicians. An example of this behavior is the attempt of private car services to operate within low-income and inner-city communities.

In urban and minority communities, taxicab service was not available. Licensed taxis refused to come into minority areas because of their perception that all Black communities had a crime problem. Private car services developed as a result of such behavior. They were called gypsy cabs. Since there were no licenses for them to obtain, they were forced to provide the services in a stealth manner. This mode of business was often treated as a criminal offense; the drivers were punished and often their cars were seized by the government. Since they primarily served minority neighborhoods, it was again not a concern for the Black politicians. These car services were necessary in a community where people generally did not own cars but rather depended upon public transportation. Nonemergency trips to the hospital were often provided by car services or gypsy cabs because public transportation was unavailable at that time. The cost of ambulances was prohibitive.

When Uber first came to the market in California, they were in violation of the same numerous state and local laws regarding the use of private car services without proper licensing. Instead of being treated like criminals, Uber was able to get the government to simply change the law. By getting politicians to change the law, Uber's activity became a multibillion-dollar operation as opposed to a criminal one. This was another multibillion-dollar industry created by purchasing government favor in the regulation process.

This is how income is shifted to the hands of the rich and powerful and limited for those who seek to work hard to provide a service that is necessary. The key issue was the use of private cars to provide transportation services without having any additional licenses paid to local governments or the state. The main difference between Uber and the old car services was that the cell phone had replaced the telephone as the way to call for a car. This is an example of how the growing disparity between minorities and the rest of society in terms of income and wealth is maintained.

Gypsy cabs were developed because of the market need for car services when taxicabs refused to go into certain predominantly minority communities. People seeing market conditions and exploiting them to create jobs and employment for themselves should be commended in a free market society. If you do this within urban communities, however, they generally find some sort of code that you are in violation of.

If Black politicians do not step up to protect local business and citizens, communities are left on their own. Gypsy cabs were run by private individuals utilizing their private cars to provide transportation services to consumers. Instead of being commended for finding a market niche that created employment within the community, these individuals were penalized with fines, arrests, and confiscation of their vehicles. This was because they failed to have a license from the city in which they operated, although no such license existed.

The limitation of business development by government with the assistance of Black politicians is massive. Many industries and professions are unnecessarily required to obtain licenses to engage in standard businesses. Once again this demonstrates the complete failure of the leadership that is supposed to exist within Black America. This leadership is merely a front for the Democratic Party and serves no true purpose in the growth of Black America. In America one of the purposes of leaders is to help define the utilization of capital within its own community. When leaders' motives are self-centered, as opposed to being centered on the interests of the community,

136

they cannot effectively provide guidance on how to benefit from capital utilization.

Some have the idea that the poor and those who live below the poverty line do not pay taxes. That is grossly untrue because the percentage of taxes paid by persons in lower income brackets relative to their income is generally higher than those who make tens of millions of dollars. These taxes may come in the form of gasoline taxes, sales taxes, cigarette taxes, and other subtle regressive taxes. A regressive tax is one in which those who have less money pay a higher percentage of their income in taxes in that area than those who have more money. It is often said that there are three sure things in this world: taxes, death, and trouble. Taxes are one of the sure things in the world because taxes fund governments. As long as there are governments, there will be taxes.

What you do with your money will determine your life to a large extent. If you do not retain sufficient resources to meet unexpected problems, you will be subject to the lowest level of care or protection that is afforded in society. Among the areas that are affected by your economic situation are your legal rights, your medical treatment, and your housing. These are three major areas that are dramatically and directly affected by your ability to generate capital. The same is true for an individual and an entire community or nation.

Slavery and gangs are really about money. The gangs make large sums of money providing goods and services that are deemed illegal by the government. Slavery was an institution designed to get cheap labor in order to provide the goods and services at the highest profit for the slave owner. Many Irish originally came to the US as indentured servants for their cheap labor and desperate situation at home.

According to a 2019 article in *Black Enterprises*, 84 percent of Black Americans believe that the achievement of the American dream means financial security. The same article indicated that 33 percent of Black Americans did not have sufficient savings to cover a thirty-day crisis. A key to achieving financial success is financial literacy or understanding how money works. *The Huffington Post* reported that 20 percent of Black Americans give themselves a grade of F in regard to financial literacy. The good news is, according to the *Black Enterprises* article, 58 percent of families are actively involved in educating their children about finances. The financial literacy that is necessary to achieve financial goals is available but must be made a priority.

Chapter 7

PUBLIC INTEREST HYPOCRISY

While numerous politicians and political parties profess their interest in doing what they think is in the public interest, what we see is little more than a level of hypocrisy that is hard to beat. I will demonstrate the level of hypocrisy by providing some examples of that hypocrisy and how it showed itself in the market.

We continue to let the government pass additional laws that we hope will benefit us. That is as stupid as asking criminals to solve the crime problem. Of course they can. But why would they when they benefit from the chaos?

According to some sources, network neutrality, or simply net neutrality, is defined as the principle that internet service providers (ISPs) must treat all internet communications equally, and not discriminate or charge differently based on user, content, website, platform, application, type of equipment, source address, destination address, or method of communication. In other words, with net neutrality, ISPs may not intentionally block, slow down, or charge money for specific online content. Without net neutrality, ISPs may prioritize certain types of traffic, meter others, or potentially block traffic from specific services, while charging consumers for various tiers of service.

The latest issue of those who claim to have the public interest in mind is net neutrality. The main issue of net neutrality is whether broadband providers can alter the speed of information delivery. Although this is not an issue currently, members of Congress seek to pass legislation that would prevent the altering of internet speeds. Internet speed alteration already happens today because different systems provide different speeds. The level of speed you have is based on the price that you pay.

Many are now concerned about net neutrality. Cities like Los Angeles actively engaged in the creation of cable television monopolies, without which this issue likely wouldn't exist. The creation of cable and wireless monopolies in the 1980s is the main reason net neutrality is an issue today. Net neutrality concerns are a function of the lack of competition in the broadband market.

There are calls to reclassify ISPs as public utilities like electricity and water and for the government to regulate their behavior and activities. The Democratic Party says that they are seeking to protect your interests when they speak of controlling net neutrality. Since the owners of ISPs own the system, they would decide the criteria for internet speeds without net neutrality. Democrats are the loudest voices regarding net neutrality in Congress.

The Democratic Party didn't seem to care about net neutrality when cable television was introduced because net neutrality did not exist as an issue at that point in time. The internet did not yet exist when cable television was created. As technology changed and the ability of the wired broadband cable system became more important, the cable monopoly began to realize it could generate more revenue by controlling the most powerful form of access to internet markets: broadband.

I'm not here to argue for or against the concept of net neutrality. I am here to argue for the free market that is supposed to exist. The free market, historically, is better at controlling pricing than the government. Local corrupt governments in collusion with private industry killed the free market of cable television by creating monopolies for their friends and large contributors. The current operators merely seek to expand the power the government gave them originally when they received their monopoly license.

The net neutrality issue is an example of how the loss of rights by the citizens of South Central could potentially affect all citizens. They take the rights of the poor and expand it to the larger market. The rights of one are the rights of all, for good and bad. In our cable license case, it was okay when the rights of Black people were being taken because all the liberals and progressives supported the deprivation of the civil rights of South Central. Nothing was said about it; the media ignored it.

Broadband service could only be delivered in most markets through the cable television system that existed there. Because the wiring was relatively new, as compared to the telephone company wiring, it has sufficient bandwidth to provide fast broadband service for its customers. The government-created monopolies now had control over the speed and delivery of content through the internet and World Wide Web. This event, the breach of net neutrality standards, has not even happened and they are already seeking legislation. They are very proactive for things they believe concern them and their

141

personal and financial interests. They allowed the Black public, Black America, to get screwed, and you should not be surprised when the actions taken against the minority are subsequently projected against the majority.

The creation of monopolies in the cable television industry would eliminate competition within the broadband industry and assure the operators that they could charge whatever rates and provide whatever level of service they chose.

The Democratic Party and elected officials were strong proponents of creating monopoly cable television systems. The same people who created the monopolies are now complaining about the results of their creation. The lack of competition in the broadband market is the reason that there is concern about net neutrality. It is not a great secret that monopolies, once formed, are difficult to control and exhibit behavior that is beyond the free marketplace standards. It is very simple: they don't care what you want as long as they can obtain the level of income that they would like.

The entire net neutrality issue is based upon the fact that broadband has no competition in the marketplace. Broadband is an extension of cable television, and cable television was created as a monopoly so that there would be no competition. Now, when the monopolies have the potential to affect someone other than Black people, the Democrats have become concerned. The ability to alter or slow down the speeds of internet service for various types of programming became a concern to those who do not want any restrictions on the programming that they seek for themselves. The fact that Black America could get very little usable programming was less concerning than the potential for slowing down the programming that the rest wanted.

142

You have given up the ability to control a monopoly after you create it and its regulation is removed from you. Now the same people that created the artificial monopoly are the ones complaining about the results that should've been obvious to anyone, even the political morons who created a monopoly. Anything that goes through the wires will be controlled by the monopoly.

The city provided the framework and protection that was needed to allow monopolies to control the media and programming market. The city was able to do what no company, regardless of its size or wealth, could possibly accomplish: defend the monopoly that had been created and prohibit any further entry into the marketplace.

There were estimates done by independent organizations regarding the cost to the consumer of maintaining a monopoly versus competition in the cable television market. The study indicated monopoly service prices were 20 percent higher than the competitive market cost for the very same services. This is especially cruel in low-income areas, where the prices were unnecessarily high. Are these high prices to provide monopoly profits to friends of elected officials?

Allowing the creation of monopolies seems contradictory to the consumer advocate position the Democratic Party supposedly supports. It turns out that the government, in some circumstances, is giving control of internet speed to those unregulated monopolies, which is the same as giving them control of price and service.

The higher prices are possible because of the monopoly status of the single provider for the service. The single provider was

143

provided protection by the government to provide news and information to the public it deemed appropriate. This is not the information the community deemed appropriate because the monopoly provider did not know or care about what the community really wanted—it only provided what was most profitable for itself.

No one should be surprised by the behavior of broadband companies, which are basically cable companies or modified cable companies from the former technology era. Are they behaving unfairly? No, they are a monopoly, and that is the point of being a monopoly. Control of the market means control of the content in that market. Your electric company does not change the power of electricity based upon the location or the customer. It must remain constant and the same for all customers. The cable television monopoly is radically different because it delivers programming the company selected based upon its ability to generate income from the communities served, whether low-income or high-income communities.

Everyone must pay when unregulated monopolies are created by ignorant, corrupt, or uncaring politicians or governments. Monopolies are among the most anti-consumer vehicles in the American economy. Where is the consumer protection that the Democrats claim is their goal?

Hypocrisy is the practice of engaging in the same behavior or activity for which one criticizes another. Public interest supporters are now complaining about situations that their party created. You cannot be on both sides of the fence at the same time. Your complaints ring hollow when you are the same person who created the issues that you are complaining about. When someone creates a situation that allows for monopoly

144

control of a major piece of media, they endanger net neutrality. Net neutrality was an issue long before the internet became a standard method of communicating in America. These are the long-term effects of passing laws that restrict freedoms for the benefit of the friends and political contributors of elected officials.

The Democratic Party has long held itself up as the party that supports consumer protection. The Democratic Party has been a leader in creating unregulated monopolies in the cable television industry throughout the United States. Creating unregulated monopolies is one of the most anti-consumer activities that any group can engage in. The decision of rates and costs to the consumer is left to multinational corporations.

Derivative industries are developed by those who control the methods of distribution such as cable television. Broadband is a derivative product of the cable television industry. The derivative product was developed by the internet industry but required access to the wires controlled by the cable television industry. The ability to deliver broadband has been limited because of the wiring that is controlled, on public rights-of-way, by the cable television industry. The ability to control derivative products through its monopoly allows the cable television industry to dictate the price of broadband and its subsequent uses. The pricing of broadband is especially prohibitive for many in communities such as South Central. The inability to access the latest technology hinders the development of communities that can't use the most effective internet delivery systems. Low-income individuals are often limited to a slower and less reliable method for their internet access.

The City of Los Angeles and many other cities across the US must bear a large part of the blame for the low involvement of minorities and low-income communities with new technologies derived from the original product, cable television. Those that made decisions in the 1980s through the early 2000s must bear responsibility for the results of their behavior.

The party would not provide consumer protection for the part of the economy that needed it most: low-income working families. While it was giving away the right to free speech to their friends and large contributors, the same behavior was increasing the cost of cable television for the regular citizen. This was especially punitive in low-income and minority communities that oftentimes could not afford the price of even basic service. Then the party complained when their friends were worried about the potential effect that the monopoly would have on their lives. The extended history of anti-consumer behavior demonstrated by the Democratic Party leaves it to great question whether their consumer protection plan is really serious or just another marketing proposal.

The city got the results that should have been expected; it is basic economics. The responsibility falls to the entire Los Angeles city government, from the mayor to city council to the little minions that they control on the various boards and committees that protect their political friends.

Chapter 8

THE CALL FOR DIVERSITY

The call for diversity is an attempt to allow all parts of society to have influence over the media they consume. The call for diversity is both right and proper per the First Amendment, which affirms diversity in opinions and ideas as they relate to the citizens of this country.

Without some control over media, we do not have any control over its messages. This is not a new concept. It's been around since the invention of radio and television. Government had limited the access by the citizens of South Central to media and thereby access to the information needed for a community. This approach will continue to prevent urban minority communities from providing the information that is important within those communities. A community cannot grow responsibly without the tools that are necessary for such growth.

When people speak of diversity, they should be speaking not only of a diversity of faces but the diversity of ideas and the necessity to hear diverse voices. The diversity of ideas is the purpose of the First Amendment. Without such diversity there cannot be true freedom within a nation. The call for true diversity is not satisfied by hiring a few people, and I mean only a few from an ethnic group to fulfill a quota. That's not diversity.

Our organization sought to provide a new technology in South Central to everyone, from every race and religion. The key, which all parties agreed on, was to maintain ownership control in the hands of Black citizens who were familiar with South Central. South Central was made up not only of Black people but had a heavy Hispanic influence within it. Their economic condition was similar to the Black occupants of this community. We felt special programming was necessary for them also in order to fulfill our responsibility to the community as a whole. We did not have confidence the government would commit to performing such action, so we took it upon ourselves as independent investors to see if we could get a South Central Los Angeles cable license.

True diversity can only be accomplished when the delivery system is owned by those who seek to provide alternative views and ideas. It is these alternative views and ideas that were embraced by the founding fathers and make up the greatness of diversity in America. When 90 percent of media content in the United States is controlled by fewer than a dozen companies, there is no true diversity in the ownership of that media.

The exclusion of the Black race from ownership is the exclusion of true diversity within media in the United States. The media are a major industry of economics within the United States. The refusal to allow an entire race of people to enter into a market, the cable television market, is clearly contrary to free speech and free markets. By locking us out, the people of South Central Los Angeles who had derivative interest in the process

148

also were also locked out. This derivative interest included the production personnel and the resources necessary to provide television programming and movies we believed would be beneficial to the community we represented.

Diversity did not matter to the politicians because they did not understand that diversity of content can only be controlled by diversity of ownership. More importantly, they did not care about the programming that was being delivered to the Black community. As long as this programming did not threaten their little jobs, they were content with it.

Despite the great number of talented Black people available in Hollywood to produce programming in 1980, no one was able to fully utilize their talent because we had no method of distributing their product. Without the ability to have your product distributed and targeted to a minority audience, programming can't be made because there is no available capital in the market for that product. Access to the information that was important to Black Americans was denied them because others would decide what was important to them and thereby provide the programming that would be consumed in Black communities. Programming directed toward the Black community would also open up potential international uses for that same programming in places such as the Virgin Islands and Africa, but opportunities to develop that programming were denied.

Nothing can truly change content diversity except a diversity of ownership. Seeking short-term solutions to long-term problems doesn't help. Bringing attention to these long-term problems has been stymied by a lack of access to media by minority citizens, up until the present. Without the ability to access and deliver the message to the minority community you represent, you cannot expect diversity to have anything more than a minimal effect—on the development of content needed by minority communities.

Unlike other metropolitan areas, Los Angeles and Hollywood specifically had numerous highly trained minority people involved in the production of content for television and movies. This included actors, actresses, producers, directors, and the technical people necessary to make production happen. Although they were capable of producing content, they had no distribution or platform for what they created.

Because Los Angeles was a center for content development, underutilizing the existing talent would hamper effective content development by Black America for decades to come. Access to both a cable license and the necessary talent and crews was part of our plan to develop Black-controlled media and content within the South Central community. Many highly capable content developers were locked out of the market, and the opportunity was lost.

The media have gotten us to believe that the most important form of diversity is diversity in entertainment programming. They portray lurid images of mass murder, rape, and other negative forms of behavior to represent Black America. That is the most profitable for them.

Not only is it important to portray positive images of Black America, there is also a great need for educational programming as opposed to entertainment programming for our community. Educational programming could provide opportunities for a community and a race to improve themselves, as discussed in Chapter 3.

Educational programming in areas such as health care, early childhood development, high school tutoring, and economics and finance would be beneficial for the South Central community and beyond. The only way this improvement can be accomplished is through the use of media, which has sufficient coverage and capability to reach the target market of Black and low-income communities. The cost of education as compared to the law enforcement alternative is minimal.

There can be no treatment for an illness for which there has been no diagnosis. The willingness of school systems to simply ignore the overt symptoms of PTSD in urban and minority schools means that there can be no resources applied to resolving this issue. Without proper diagnosis there can be no treatment, and without treatment there can be no solution.

There can be no diagnosis on a community-wide basis when there are no resources for the communication of problems within your own community. Mass media allow you to reach mass audiences. These audiences often have unique problems that are overlooked, like most problematic things in minority communities.

Electronic communication systems for consumers are known as mass media. First radio, then television, then cable television— now the internet offers a new method of broad interface. The speed of change in this digital age gives me some solace that media and information access may come to Black America sooner than cable television came to South Central.

Cable television companies are now leading owners of the programming displayed on the cable television systems they own. The monopolists are now some of the leading providers of content that goes into the monopoly cable television systems.

Most major cable television companies own at least 10 percent of the providers that are carried on their system.

It does not matter how many Black faces you see on TV. Ultimately, they can only say and do things that are acceptable to the owners. Actors and directors are all subject to the approval and consent of the media owner. Cable provided an opportunity for true diversity that could have produced numerous jobs in the programming and content sectors, especially in Los Angeles.

My entire family was excited when the first television shows starring Black leads were put on television in the 1960s. This was the beginning of diversity in television. One of the first shows featuring a Black performer was the variety show *Sammy Davis, Jr. Show*, which first aired in 1966. In 1968 the first dramatic series with a Black lead was titled *Julia* starring Diahann Carroll. In the show she played a widowed single mother who was a registered nurse. The dramatic nature of the show was a unique feature that brought great pride to Black America.

Yet from the beginning of the millennium many of the shows featuring Black performers are what is called "reality programming." These shows are no more a reality than cartoons like *Bugs Bunny*. They are fantasies, not realities. They follow continuing confrontations among people, and when there is no confrontation, the producers make sure that a confrontation is created nonetheless.

There are is array of Black "reality" shows depicting rude, overdressed, and ignorant people who are supposed to be representative of the bulk of Black America, which they are not. They have almost nothing to do with reality. Black youth

152

use these shows as guidance for their behavior. Their concept of reality is distorted because television keeps telling them these shows are what they should strive for in reality.

These shows range from *Real Housewives of Atlanta* to *Love & Hip Hop*. Their commonality is an extremely high-income group of Black people, generally displaying bizarre and aberrant behavior that is filtered down to teenagers and children because they see it on television. Young people believe this vulgar display of wealth is somehow representative of what they should be doing and what is going on in terms of Black people. It is a complete distortion of the reality of Black America. It reinforces that conspicuous consumption is better because it gives you the appearance of having wealth, as opposed to actually having wealth.

It is completely unrealistic to believe people spend their lives under the vision of constant cameras, producers, and other workers necessary to produce a "reality" television show. The mere fact that these production personnel are present indicates this cannot be reality. When was the last time you had a camera crew in your living room or in your office following you around to see what you were doing? Maybe that's the attraction of the show, but it has nothing to do with reality.

With no competing Black television, there is no media to contradict what they call reality programming. Getting information based upon these shows distorts what life is truly like. Programming contradicting these shows, or at least showing an alternative lifestyle, is not allowed. In Black America, we want to live the hero lifestyle of the rich and famous. Maybe we need to spend some time with the poverty lifestyle—the lifestyle one-quarter of Black America really lives. Now that's reality.

The public believes what they see on these shows somehow constitutes a viable expectation of the behavior of Black people. The public believes this level of continuous confrontation is the standard of behavior within urban communities. Do we want to present that kind of picture? Do we want the behavior within communities to mimic the behavior shown on these television shows, glorified by media, and given substantial exposure to the general public?

When it comes to the development of content, it's important to repair those misrepresentations; otherwise, Black America cannot prosper in line with the rest of the society. Because we do not control the media and cannot deliver a message we are trying to portray, we are unable to provide the information we deem appropriate for our own children, communities, and place in society.

The view of Black America by Black Americans is often a negative one. There are many reasons why we have a negative view of ourselves. This is partially due to the negative images that are continually portrayed in the media. The view provided to all of America is the same that Black Americans get to see as we try to interpret who we are. Black-on-Black crime at the street level is a manifestation of Black-on-Black crime at the political level. No one would expect the law to resolve their differences in South Central. The law is looked at as an enemy by many. Local government has shown itself to be dishonest and not to be relied upon to find a just solution to your issues. Black-on-Black crime is a major problem in Black America, and yet we look for answers to that problem somewhere else, outside of Black America. The lack of diversity of content allows for misinformation to go unchallenged in the media because those whose images are being tarnished have no access

154

to control of the media. There must be alternative views for areas with problems significantly different from those of the broad spectrum of society. Without the ability to express views and seek answers to questions there can be no solutions, as you can see with the current status of Black America.

A long-running show demonstrating a negative view of Black America is the television show *Cops*. The show is filmed from a number of different cities and follows police officers engaged in the arrest or chasing of African-Americans for some crime, either real or perceived. The continual demonstration of Black Americans as criminals reinforces the stereotype for the American audience, including the Black American audience. These ongoing negative impressions are reinforced with no contradictory programming to show the true side of Black America. It appears that any police misconduct is simply left on the cutting-room floor of the production room. This does not give a true and fair representation of Black America or the police, especially considering the experiences of Black Americans in South Central Los Angeles.

Shows such as the *Jerry Springer Show* depict Black Americans in a negative light by calling it reality programming. On one episode there was a teenage Black girl who claimed to be trying to find the father of her daughter. They tested fourteen different men, and none of them turned out to be the father of this child. The fact that this young girl had sexual contact with more than fourteen people within a two-week period indicates her low self-esteem, at the very least.

Her fifteen minutes of fame were very harsh in front of the entire viewing audience. Did anyone advise this young lady before she decided to go on the show? The fact that the *Jerry*

155

Springer Show has existed for so long indicates many Black Americans will watch anything featuring a Black face.

An understanding of Black America can never be achieved by looking at these shows. But these are the shows broadcast. This is not diversity; it is an egregious misrepresentation of Black America.

The reality of Black America is not represented on television because the media and technology have been withheld from those who can accurately and fairly display true life in Black America. The great thing is that technology continually changes, and new opportunities present themselves.

The new technology and most available method of distribution of available content is now streaming. This is media delivered through the internet without the need for additional wires or antennas to bring such programming to your home or portable device. All major media companies have a substantial presence in the streaming market. New companies such as Netflix have made this medium their full delivery system.

Black Americans should be looking at streaming as an opportunity to provide content programming for their own community. Urban and minority communities do not need any more programming that is entertainment. They need programming that is educational, informational, and entertaining by representing the true lives of Black America.

Chapter 9

A STORY OF BLACK AMERICA TODAY

E veryone has a story, so they say. We know that stories change as they are passed through people. A story repeated four times never comes out the same as when it started. If that story is then told to the original storyteller, they will probably not recognize it. Whose voice tells the story of Black America? It is clear that it is not Black America.

When any group of people cannot tell their own story, it must be told by someone who does not know exactly what goes on within that group. This is where we are in America today. The image of Black America is made by the rest of America, not by Black America. The story of Indians in America is an example of that distortion. It is the victor who tells the story in any battle or skirmish or war. If someone is interpreting your story, what you have is an interpretation of a story, not the story itself. There can be a vast difference between the real version and the imagined version.

It is not the Black people themselves who tell their own story but others who give you their interpretation of the story.

Those without sufficient knowledge to create a valid image of minority communities often provide an incorrect vision of those communities.

There are two major cable networks whose programming is directed toward the Black community. They are Black Entertainment Television (BET) and the Oprah Winfrey Network (OWN). BET was formed in 1980 and originally provided news and informational programming in addition to entertainment programming. BET is not owned by Black people; rather, it is a subsidiary of Viacom. Around 1992, BET eliminated all news and informational programming and focused exclusively on entertainment. People such as Tavis Smiley, who had a successful and popular program on BET, would have to move to other stations—PBS in Smiley's case— in order to continue to provide meaningful insight for the Black community.

OWN was created in 2011 by Oprah Winfrey as an alternative or supplement to the programming provided by BET. The iconic status of Oprah Winfrey encouraged major cable television companies to carry this channel. OWN carries less entertainment programming than BET but provides more original and informational programming. While there are other smaller networks in the marketplace, none has been able to gain the standing of OWN or BET. I believe that the reason they cannot effectively compete is the lack of capital to develop programming. The major programming carried by BET is reruns of old television shows and movies. The deep pockets of Viacom allow them to acquire preexisting programming for their network.

The public depends on media, be it cable or internet, to get their information about what goes on in society. If the nature of minorities is misrepresented in these forums, then the general public is not capable of effectively evaluating the authenticity or truthfulness of the information being put forward about that minority. If you cannot validate the information, it is more difficult to rely on it. Those who rely on unvalidated information are more likely to ignore the true effect of what goes on in our society.

Media portray the extremes of society, not the normal behavior in society every day. A man biting a dog is news, but a dog biting a man is not news. A lot more men are bitten by dogs than dogs by men. In the same way, media also portray the unusual, not the normal, behavior of minorities by showing them engaged in criminal behavior or some sort of aberrant behavior. These images portrayed in media are often accepted by those minorities who are being misrepresented because it is the only information available to those without access to or control of media.

The ability to freely establish your own image is an important part of being an American. Before the domination of media, we learned from our parents and in our neighborhood. For example, attending church with our families and interacting with older, wiser adults gave us values we could cherish in the real world. Now, the image we see of ourselves is the image given to us by media and we pay more attention to screens of various sizes than we do people.

These media are not controlled by us, the minority communities. So we must be concerned about the effects of these distortions on our minority communities and the communities seeing these distorted portrayals.

Media make their money by presenting extremes as opposed to the regular parts of the American way of life. Media are more concerned with presenting images of civil disobedience. Media spend much less time discussing the causes of such civil disobedience as opposed to the result. In order for low-income and minority communities to understand the root causes of their discontent and civil disobedience, they need to understand the basic structure and systems of the society from which they have been excluded.

You may not want to hear what I've got to say. That is okay, but I'm going to say it anyway. Black Americans are almost as afraid of Black Americans as White Americans are. Black-on-Black crime is a standard part of low-income and minority communities. Most crimes that have Black victims also have Black perpetrators. This does not lead to great trust within our own community.

Losing the protection of the First Amendment rights guaranteed to citizens by the Constitution is a precursor to the deprivation of additional constitutional rights. Black America and White America are concerned about government actions that ignore the Constitution and instead substitute laws that limit our constitutional rights.

No other group of people is allowed to use a derogatory term about their own people while being supported by media to such an extent that the word has become commonplace. Is there some power in only Black people using the N-word? Is that the real reason for using it? When there is no chance to counteract the effect of derogatory terms used against you, the effect of its use will be magnified—positively, to some within your groups, but negatively among other groups.

Without media, you cannot explain the great suffering this word has caused Black people for the last two centuries. You gain much perspective about an issue to be able to understand the history of it. The widespread use of the N-word by Black entertainers can indicate a disrespect of the history of Black America, but at the same time, Black Americans want other ethnic groups to respect the history of Black America. The widespread use of the N-word is one of many problems facing Black America. Those who teach through music and media and make use of derogatory terms like the N-word to describe our people are glorified by the media and made rich. Every person using the word should have to explain to their audience the history of the word and its meaning in America over the last two centuries.

I have been called the N-word by a Black government official in the office of Mayor Bradley in Los Angeles City Hall. When Black government officials start calling you names, you realize the problem you're going to have pursuing your goals of community empowerment. Can I realistically criticize entertainers who use the word when it was used by a Black official working for the City of Los Angeles? I don't care whether it's a politician or policeman calling me that name—it is still grossly offensive to me and certainly contrary to how government officials should treat citizens. The behavior demonstrated by elected officials in City Hall showed a complete lack of respect for our efforts, for the South Central community, and for their citizens. When that sort of derogatory comment is made in

City Hall, I can't have any expectation that the police force will have a different attitude toward the residents of South Central.

It is unrealistic to use the word on a continual basis and then believe you can keep other people in society from using the word. Wake up and smell the coffee. You just don't get it if you think that's how a worldwide audience, influenced by worldwide media, is going to react. The word denigrates, to an entire nation and the world, the effect and the memory of its tragic meaning. Many things, good and bad, can happen with the use of a single word.

Promoting and allowing the broad use of derogatory terminology used to denigrate the lives of Black Americans for hundreds of years is part of the reason for a lack of understanding beyond Black America and the lack of self-respect within the Black community. I feel that our hatred of this word is deeply ingrained in Black America and we hurt ourselves as a race by using it.

How many men and women have lost their lives while people screamed the word over them? The pervasive use of the word minimizes its true meaning. But as long as media companies all over the United States are making money on hip-hop and gangsta rap that disrespects the history of Black America, and as long as it comes out of our own mouths, the disrespect will stay alive—one N-word at a time. The serious nature of the use of the word is indicated to me because it seems to me that more law enforcement officers lose their jobs for using the N-word as opposed to excessive use of force against Black people.

We must educate our children and promote the moral values we deem appropriate and important. Each part of society has its own needs, and the needs of Black America are different than the needs of other parts of society. Dr. Martin Luther King Jr. said, "Intelligence plus character—that is the goal of true education." In the modern world we cannot develop character or values without access to and control of media.

The idea of Black people trying to blame someone else for our problems is ridiculous. We had better take a close look in the mirror to see what our responsibility is as we try to progress as a race of people and as members of a society. Of course there is racism, and it will continue to some extent as long as there are races. As long as there are differences within human beings, there will be those who seek to exploit those differences and to make themselves feel they are better than others. I can truly say that no racism has damaged me more, in my pursuits as a Black man, than the racism perpetrated by Black politicians. Not the usual offender when a Black man talks about racism.

Many races and religions have faced discrimination, many for longer times than the Black experience in America. Many races and religions have assimilated into America despite early discrimination, including Jews and Italians. Our skin color means assimilating into American culture cannot be done by just simply changing our name and not making an issue of our background. Black America cannot do this.

Drugs, legal and illegal, consume a higher percentage of the disposable income in Black America than in the rest of America, but the disposable income of the average Black American is substantially lower than that of other Americans. The waste of this capital, both monetary and human, could solve at least some of the problems that plague our urban and minority communities. The American economy and most other economies are built on being able to get enough money together to reach financial and personal goals. Very few people have the capital to fund their own ideas and dreams. By seeking capital from investors and related parties, individuals are able to achieve the formation of an idea into a reality. This knowledge and the opportunities it represents are not readily available in minority communities.

If we can solve half of our own problems, why not do it? Let us be more concerned about options in our own control instead of relying solely on the government. It has become quite clear in the last forty years that the government cannot be the primary source for the solution of problems within the Black community. They continually pass new laws to penalize Black people couched in supposed concern for criminal activity and supporting the best interests of the Black community.

Much of America has adopted various Black influences on behavior and language that have become part of the fabric of our society. In language, the use of words such as brother and dope have become a part of the American lexicon. Such Black behaviors as "slapping five" or "giving each other skin" have become common in American behavior. There is no reason why we should not take advantage of this assimilation in terms of business.

Great disappointment within the Black community leads to a lack of respect for the members within the community, which triggers crimes in order to gain respect through violence. This is part of the gang mentality. The "thug life" mentality has grown and reinforced itself because of the lack of competing ideas and thoughts that could offer other outlets to these disenfranchised young men and women within the community.

Why do we disrespect ourselves? Could it be we are missing the necessary mentors? I was very fortunate to have two good parents who gave me and my five siblings an understanding of what my path could be within American society. They did not depend on schools, gangs, peers, or media to provide those insights; they did it themselves.

But what happens when parents are not capable of or willing to provide the information and assistance their children need to grow into responsible adults? I believe the proliferation of single-parent families without adequate mentoring assistance in war zone conditions has contributed to the lack of parental influence on children's lives. That void is often filled, in urban minority communities, by gangs and negative media. Gangs provide protection and economic stimuli, although illegal, to those who are unsure of any other way to gain footing and respect in a society that seems to have marginalized their importance and benefit to society.

Government has become an unwanted partner with parents in child-rearing, making rules and laws determining how you raise and discipline your children. Should the government then also take responsibility for the high failure rate, on so many levels? In California, in some cases parents must pay part of their children's incarceration fees while the children are sentenced to juvenile detention facilities. Police officers, agents of the government, may discipline your child as they deem appropriate, without any concern for what is necessary or legal. The police may kick, shoot, throw your child to the ground, cuff them and have them sit on a curb, and engage in any other behavior they deem appropriate. No parent could treat their children the way agents of the government treat our children and not be subject to severe criminal prosecution.

This is not only for children or young adults who are engaged in criminal activity or have been violating laws. In New York, the police enforcement of the stop and frisk statute meant that any policeman could stop any Black person in order to search them for weapons or contraband. In this process, numerous innocent children were slammed to the ground and slammed into walls by groups of large men with guns and badges. Is the treatment more humane when the abuser has a gun and a badge? Any resistance to this behavior was considered obstructing a police officer or resisting arrest. You did not need to be charged with a crime to be charged with resisting arrest.

In 1990, the City of Los Angeles decided to change the name of South Central Los Angeles to simply South Los Angeles. This was done because of the negative connotation the name South Central created in people outside of the City of Los Angeles. This is once again the concept of image over reality. The city fathers thought they would change the reality of South Central Los Angeles by merely changing its name to South Los Angeles. These people and their ideas are the ones leading us. They don't care about changing the reality; they only care about changing the perception.

The failure of government to provide alternative avenues for those who are in need has led to a dangerous situation. There is a shadow government existing in Black communities: gangs. They rule the community with violence and possess the weaponry to supply a small army. The average citizen is powerless against these gangs because they have neither the resources nor the ability to combat them. They often find their own children entangled in these gangs because gangs have gained a certain degree of legitimacy among young people who feel they have been excluded from the rest of society. These

166

gangs have access to money from their illegal activities, which becomes extremely impressive to young people, who are taught money is the most important thing in America and to ignore the possible prison time such allegiances may cost them in the future. The allure of the thug life, by dress and/or behavior, is very tempting, but it makes them targets of law enforcement, as well.

The phenomenal rates of incarceration of young Black people is part of a deep betrayal of the Black community going on in South Central each and every day. Locking juveniles in cages and subjecting them to psychopaths and torture doesn't correct their antisocial behavior.

As I see it, the prison system is merely a training ground for petty criminals to become full-fledged gang members and deadly criminals. Often incarcerations are usually for an extreme number of years. Unfair and extreme sentencing is a violation of the Equal Protection Clause of the Fourteenth Amendment. This clause is supposed to guarantee equal treatment by the law, even for violations of law. Another piece of the Constitution discarded.

Substantial parts of the Black population are caught up in a war zone. These war zones were created based upon the war on drugs that has been directed against the citizens of the United States. Like any war zone, there are rules of engagement, and those rules of engagement tend to follow military procedures as opposed to civilian police procedures. The rules of engagement allow for substantial collateral damage to citizens that were not involved in any illegal activity but merely exist in a war zone. We are refusing to label urban communities war zones, even when people are killed each week with military weapons by

167

warring military factions. The refusal of elected officials to acknowledge the truth does not solve the problem; it merely covers it up for the rest of society, but not for those who live in the war zone. There are also disputes among gangs as they try to obtain additional markets and revenues.

Young people created their own media with hip-hop and rap music. This music focuses on some of the negative forces within our society and minimizes any positive circumstances that may exist. Without counterbalancing positive influences in relation to this art form, there is no method for the community to positively influence its own children.

Gangsta rap was developed by inner-city residents as a form of expression for their unique situation. It elevates those that would expect their counterparts to have criminal convictions and prison time. You cannot fault people for telling you what they see within their own lives and communities. Young hip-hop artists were able to take advantage of the capitalist system by producing and selling products independent of media sources by selling at the shows where they were performing. This is an example of how industries are created in a free market. These rappers are in fact capitalists. Their ability to distribute their music, independent of the media, was an important step in the development of this music type. They have an interest in a multimillion-dollar industry.

People often wonder why there is such a high unemployment rate in the Black community. A substantial reason is that Black Americans have been locked out of the job market— some say for more than two hundred years, while others laud the improvements for many Black Americans in our country since the civil rights movement. But discrimination, drugs, war zone environments, gangs, and the lack of higher education opportunities have impacted Black youth.

How do people learn to work? They learn from example and gain work habits from parents, mentors, or time on the job. Young people often learn the benefit of work habits from their parents. But unemployment, incarceration, and drug addiction create a system of poverty under which many Black Americans live. Instead of being employed, parents and role models are criminalized for being poverty-stricken because there are no jobs available. Blacks, at times, by situation and circumstance, are locked out of education and therefore the benefits that go with it. A criminal record reduces your chances of getting a legal job. Vagrancy laws and other laws relating to homelessness keep you from obtaining a job. Children cannot learn skills from parents if those parents are barred from employment. They are now caught in the welfare system.

The criminalization of poverty has been an ongoing situation for Black America since their emancipation in the 1800s. The most glaring example of this is the vagrancy laws that existed from emancipation through the 1960s. These laws allowed local governments and police departments to take people off the streets if they did not have a visible means of support. As a newly freed slave, you could not provide a visible means of support. For their jail sentence, they were often leased back to the slaveholders they had left as part of the emancipation process. Local law enforcement acted as a procurer of what was essentially slave labor. The ability to criminalize poverty and incarcerate those who had no ability to participate in the economy was an attempt to reinstitute a form of slavery.

If a homeless person passes out on the street, it is a crime. The crime is poverty. Homelessness is sometimes a result of excessive drug or and alcohol use. It does not matter, when you're living on the street, whether a substance is legal or illegal. You're generally trying to cope with the situation, which is often dangerous.

There are numerous laws against sleeping on sidewalks or loitering, but, as a homeless person, you have nowhere to go and nothing to do. You have no place of residence, nothing to do, no income, and you are out on the streets. So the fact is that your crime is really poverty, and your illegal action, like urinating in public, is due to your lack of residence and bathrooms open to you. In the law, when there is no allowance for such circumstances and behavior, you criminalize them. Is this a mere excuse to keep the prisons filled with expensively housed poor and mentally ill people?

People of color make up a substantially higher portion of the incarcerated population in the United States. Compared with White people, their sentence is longer for the same crime, and they are disproportionately sentenced to death for their crimes. In the criminal justice system, racial disparities also threaten people of color by disenfranchising ex-convicts and limiting opportunities for housing and employment when they get out of jail or prison. In light of these disparities, it is imperative that criminal justice issues continue to be included in the major civil rights battle of the twenty-first century.

Every day, thousands of Black men are turned over to corporations to be held on behalf of the government. These people have been sentenced to prisons owned not by the government but rather by private companies that make substantial amounts of money incarcerating prisoners.

The government is different than corporations. The government is not in the *business* of incarcerating people but rather incarcerates them pursuant to the laws of the country or state. Profit-making enterprises such as private prisons determine what level of care and custody they will use for the convicts they have been given by the state. Their goal as a profit-making enterprise is to maximize their profits, not to make improvements for those who are incarcerated under their control. The use of private prisons encourages extended incarceration because of the potential profit. Now that there are privately owned prisons, will there also be a privately owned corporate police force to patrol the cities of this nation?

Private prisons have been shown to have a higher rate of recidivism of those released than people who were incarcerated in government-controlled facilities. One of the reasons, it has been reported, is that private prison personnel have less training and experience than personnel in government-controlled facilities. The for-profit facilities are more violent both for prisoners and guards.

In 2008, a Pennsylvania juvenile court judge was indicted for taking bribes in exchange for sentencing juveniles to a private detention facility. The judge would sentence juveniles to six months to one year in juvenile custody for things as insignificant as criticizing an assistant principal on the internet. This became known as the "kids for cash" scandal. The owner of the juvenile detention facility was paying the judge to sentence children to his facility so that he could make more money. I would seriously doubt that this is the only circumstance in which this behavior is taking place. The judge was sentenced to twenty-eight years in prison for having destroyed the futures of more than 2,000 children.

This is what happens when the profit motive is installed in the criminal justice system.

The private prison industry is a $70 billion per year industry. Corrections Corporation of America, the nation's largest private prison system, has more than 100,000 inmates in its control. It would appear that those who profit from incarceration would seek to keep convicts incarcerated longer. The private prison industry lobbies on both a state and federal level to make their support of longer prison sentences known.

Incarceration has become a profitable private enterprise to take control of those who are mentally ill and not able to care for themselves. As opposed to $50,000 per year to incarcerate a person, the cost of $12,000 per year to treat a person seems like a much better deal for society. In addition, it leaves more prison room for those who actually need to be imprisoned. Prison was intended for those criminals who were violent and exhibited extremely aberrant behavior such that would threaten general members of society.

After the 1992 Los Angeles riots, the causes of incarceration identified by numerous politicians included homelessness, unemployment, and frustration of inner-city youth. The *LA Times* quoted Maxine Waters, whose district included most of South Central, as saying, "I have to believe that not only can we change things, but that I can contribute to that." In 2020, as we evaluate the problems within South Central, homelessness, unemployment, and frustration of inner-city youth are once again identified as major causes of the problems. What has changed since 1992?

This is my story and my view. I speak for no one other than myself and those whom I had the privilege to represent during the battle for the civil rights guaranteed to us under the Bill of Rights. I have not received the vote of any citizen to speak for them.

Chapter 10

JUVENILE PTSD

G rown men and women are shipped off to war with the expectation to see people killed and to kill people. People going into the military should have some expectations of seeing, and possibly experiencing, extreme violence in their tours of duty. But they have training to deal with combat situations. That is the nature of the military. Some of these men and women, after experiencing active combat, develop PTSD: posttraumatic stress disorder. PTSD can also affect people who have experienced or witnessed a terrifying, life-threatening, or traumatic event.

While we widely associate PTSD with warfare and military conflict, PTSD is very prevalent in violent urban communities in the United States. Certain communities are equivalent to war zones. The number of people killed and wounded per 100,000 citizens is often higher in urban and minority low-income communities than in overseas war zones involving the US military. The 1 per 100,000 number is the standard measuring procedure for calculating the total effect of violence upon the population, either at war or in civil circumstances.

PTSD existed long before it was even understood at the military level. PTSD has been in the Black community for many years because of the level of violence that exists within low-income and inner-city communities. The circumstances that create PTSD are continually displayed there.

PTSD diagnoses in the military are relatively new. In previous wars, it was called shell shock or battle fatigue. PTSD is a disorder of a mental capacity that is brought about by traumatic and/or violent experiences that are difficult to deal with.

Witnessing violence is a major cause of PTSD. One of the effects of PTSD is the disruption of cognitive growth. Living in a war zone, such as many urban environments resemble today, makes it easy for the symptoms to manifest themselves in the general public. Gangs are set up and armed as military units. This is one of the reasons why certain communities are called war zones. The inner-city resident is subject to violence by gangs willing to use whatever is necessary to accomplish their means, including military-level munitions. They are engaged in the war for drugs, money, and territory, fought between a militarized police force and various militarized gangs.

Witnessing extreme violence in childhood, including murders, assaults, and gunfights, scars young and impressionable minds. These children can neither understand nor rationalize the behavior causing the situation, so ingrained fear, which is a precursor to mental illness, sometimes plagues these children into adulthood.

Soldiers know what they're getting into when they join the marines or the army and are sent to Iraq and Afghanistan to fight in a war. It is ridiculous to expect a juvenile, six or ten years old, with no intention of involving themselves in violent behavior, to be able to deal with such issues in an urban warfare setting. It is clear that extensive mental health resources must be spent in these communities to alleviate juvenile PTSD. Unfortunately, urban violence is rarely mentioned in conjunction with a mental illness and/or violent behavior after the fact.

Some of the signs of PTSD include feeling upset by things that remind you of what happened, nightmares or flashbacks of the event that make you feel like it's happening all over again, feeling emotionally cut off from others, feeling constantly on guard, feeling irritated, and experiencing angry outbursts that can lead to paranoia, schizophrenia, sociopathic behavior, and drug abuse in later years, if gone undiagnosed and untreated. When the illness has a dramatic effect upon the entire family of the affected individual, there is a ripple effect throughout the entire community.

These symptoms are well recognized in the urban educational environment. The symptoms are displayed by the youth in the urban educational environment, and the disruptive effect of this behavior takes a toll on all students within that educational environment. Therefore, it is not unusual that low performance scores in inner-city schools correlate with the high incidence of young people witnessing violence.

These urban war zone communities do not have access to general medical care, much less the greatly needed mental health services. In many low-income and minority communities, students with undiagnosed and untreated PTSD are penalized for their antisocial behavior the illness generates. Parents are often not able to recognize the indicators of such an illness because they are not trained to uncover their child's problem. Undiagnosed children are being penalized for illness.

When even an organization with resources like the Veterans Health Administration has trouble dealing with PTSD patients, it's clear that PTSD is a serious issue in our society. As the institution in charge of giving physical and mental health care to veterans, they are aware of the specific issues of PTSD and are attempting to provide services in order to treat the disorder. The level of resources available to organizations such as the VA greatly dwarfs anything available to the general population for the same illness. This is especially true in urban and minority areas, where residents often have no health insurance or low-level health insurance that does not provide for mental health treatments. Although PTSD has a higher level of occurrence within minority communities than in the rest of society, there is little, if any, treatment available for this disorder.

I suggest this is an issue for very large and well-funded organizations to confront. There must be identification or a reallocation of resources in order to address mental illness in the inner city, especially PTSD in juveniles. The behavior of those with PTSD has an effect upon the entire community.

It is important to remember that the symptoms of PTSD can be misdiagnosed in youth because of their overlap with behaviors common to adolescents. In communities where this illness is known to have taken hold, it is important for it to be treated as an epidemic that has infected the entire community.

What do you think the effects of PTSD are for those who have no concept of what it is and have not volunteered to participate in any dangerous or deadly situations? Undiagnosed PTSD for children as young as eight years old through their middle teens results in mental illness later in life for many.

It has been estimated that more than one-third of youths who are exposed to community violence (for example, a shooting, stabbing, or other assault) will suffer from PTSD at some time. Since violence is so prevalent in Black communities, it is highly likely that a very high percentage of Black youth who live in the inner city are suffering from some form of PTSD.

Childhood PTSD often results in meeting the criminal justice system as opposed to the medical system. Police are not trained to be mental health experts, trying to resolve mental health issues in their short interactions with the affected person. PTSD can also be caused by traumatic and violent interactions with the local police force in urban and inner-city areas. The affected are thus afraid to interface with police under almost any conditions. This fear of the police force is an excellent tool for the gangs to recruit and enhance their population. The young people feel a certain degree of safety by being in a gang because of the protection they are afforded within the local geographic area.

In addition to those risk factors, children, adolescents, females, members of minority groups, and people with learning disabilities or domestic violence in the home seem to have a greater risk of developing PTSD after a traumatic event.

Children with PTSD don't have a chance in society because they are criminalized, sometimes by the age of twelve. The criminalization of mental illness in youth will scar them for life, with criminal records hindering their ability to enter schools and seek employment. By compromising the potential of a PTSD-afflicted child, you increase the chances of police run-ins and incarceration, decrease their ability to generate the income in later life necessary to maintain them, and increase family and community problems.

The problem of PTSD is a function of being forced to live in a war zone. Soldiers do not get PTSD in training but in real combat situations. Every day is a real combat situation in many Black communities. Their lives are not one-year deployments, but a lifetime deployment that often cannot be escaped with the limited resources available.

The additional stress put on the police with dealing with those who suffer from PTSD is as unfair to them as to the citizens with the illness. A mental illness should be treated in a medical situation, not a police situation. Expansion of mental health care could reduce police involvement with those who are mentally ill. The job of the police is not to cure the mentally ill. Their job does involve interacting with mentally ill people, but it is not supposed to be their primary responsibility. Medical care also provides an alternative to the expensive process of incarceration in prisons.

Once again, the allocation of resources determines the outcome within a given community. When your leadership ignores a major mental illness prevalent within your community and there are no resources provided for the resolution of that problem, the problem simply gets worse. As demonstrated by the VA's attempts to treat veterans with PTSD, the problem requires significant resources. Yet Black America, as before, must depend upon someone else to make their issues known to the public.

It has become clear in recent years that PTSD leads to criminal behavior, aggression, and additional mental illnesses such as paranoia, schizophrenia, and suicide starting at a very young age. It is not realistic to expect ten-year-old children to deal with this issue without assistance. Millions of young Black boys and girls are suffering from a traumatic illness that brings down grown men and women who were more prepared to see violence.

Those children displaying PTSD-like behavior are often either ignored or disciplined for the aberrant behavior that is not fully within their control. This only treats the symptoms, the negative behavior, and not the illness. Classroom disruption decreases educational achievement because educational resources, rather than medical ones, are required to deal with this mental disorder. Teachers can report suspected child abuse. Why can no one recognize or report cases of PTSD in their classrooms?

The unwillingness to address a serious illness that is widespread within a community can only lead to more negative consequences. The individual is impacted because they are ill and do not know they are ill. They are not receiving a correct diagnosis and treatment. The entire community is impacted by the uncontrollable or bizarre behavior of those suffering from PTSD. The illness may manifest itself in a number of different ways.

Inner-city young people sometimes have a lower expectation of our society. This lower expectation gives them fewer incentives to take the steps necessary to achieve their goals. Why try?

In a low-income community with a poor education system there are few resources available to exit your current situation.

It is certainly not the world that appears on television under the guise of Black reality shows.

Many young Black men live with the expectation that they will end up in prison at some point in their lives. They do not expect fair treatment in the criminal justice system. It is not a place to resolve juvenile PTSD or any form of mental illness, let alone the ongoing rapes and violence that are the norm in prison, a serious matter not dealt with here. I urge people to look at the treatment people receive in prisons and to consider prison reform issues.

Abuse of drugs and alcohol is not an unusual problem with PTSD. It is normal and expected behavior for a certain portion of those with the illness as they try to self-medicate to relieve their symptoms. People use illegal drugs for the same reason they use legal drugs such as alcohol and tobacco. They dull the senses and alter feelings and focus.

Those suffering from untreated PTSD are dangerous to themselves and those around them. Those with mental illness can inflict injury, harm, and death upon those who come into contact with them if both parties are not prepared.

Group behavior in gangs is partly based upon the depersonalization or devaluing of people who are not part of the gang. In these conditions gang members feel justified in shooting into a crowd of twelve children because they are mad at one person within the crowd. These other children are no longer human beings but merely objects in the way of the gang members' goals. Their goal is the termination of the person they seek—abnormal behavior within a normal society but acceptable to inner-city gangs.

As you might imagine, Black leadership does not even begin to understand or show a concern for such behavior or such disorders that exist within the community. Such disorders are inevitable within a community that has a substantial problem with violence, poverty, and self-destructive behavior. Ignoring the problem will not solve or bring resolution any more than it would for any other illness, mental or physical.

It is the responsibility of qualified medical personnel to develop a program for the evaluation and treatment of this illness as an epidemic in urban and minority schools. If this were measles, whatever resources were necessary would be applied to resolve the issue.

There is a trade-off between increased funds for mental health care and the reduction of funds necessary to maintain such a substantial level of incarceration, especially among young Black men. By treating people for a mental illness earlier, society can avoid the need for a more costly intervention with police and prisons. No nation incarcerates a higher percentage of its population than the United States. I believe the failure to offer treatment for mental illness plays a part in this high incarceration rate. It is currently estimated that approximately 20 percent of the US prison population has some form of mental illness. As previously mentioned, the largest mental health facility in the United States is at Rikers Island prison in New York City.

This is what happens in a war zone. Parts of South Central Los Angeles were war zones during the 1980s and 1990s, especially in 1992, when military forces were called to the community in order to reestablish governmental control of the area.

Chapter 11

SUMMARY

T he City of Los Angeles, its elected officials, and its courts
have engaged in limiting the rights of Black citizens
within their control for their private benefit and that
of the Democratic Party. They have betrayed the rights and
possibilities of the citizens of South Central Los Angeles. The
deprivation of constitutional rights in Los Angeles was echoed
by the cities of Inglewood, Compton, and others. Denial of
technology was one of the cruelest things they could have done
to keep the neighborhood from becoming a part of society,
struggling to catch up with the other neighborhoods in the city
and society more broadly.

Rest assured, these are not merely allegations; there is absolute
proof of such behavior by the City of Los Angeles against my
partners and me. Our successful legal case against the city is
documented in the court records of the various federal courts
we encountered during our ten-year battle. The most adamant
and vociferous opponents to Black ownership of media within
South Central were a Black mayor, the Black city councilmen,
and the Democratic Party.

When the city finally allowed cable television to come into South Central, it was controlled by a major contributor to the Democratic Party and sold three years later without any cable being laid in South Central. The licensee sold it to another company. The City of Los Angeles was willing to give a license to their supporters, so someone friendly to the Democratic Party controlled the electronic press in South Central.

The deprivation of access to technology in the poorest community within Los Angeles was one of the most significant attacks upon African-Americans in the last fifty years. This deprivation of technology required depriving the citizens of South Central the constitutional rights provided for them in the First Amendment to the Constitution.

Without cable television, the community could not speak within its own confines about its own issues. The effects are clearly contrary to the Constitution, which is supposed to protect citizens from the government. I believe the inability of the citizens of South Central Los Angeles to communicate among themselves was a leading factor in the exponential growth of gangs within this community in subsequent years. Without competition for the minds of our youth, the gangs were able to take over with a combination of violence and financial benefits for those who would join them in their illegal enterprises. Whether these enterprises were legal or illegal was a secondary factor to those who did not see any alternative path within these communities.

Civil rights must be valid for the one and to all. Thereby attaching the entire group of people who possess common traits and whose civil rights are upheld for all the group. I point to the case of *Miranda v. Arizona* and the importance of that case

186

to all citizens within the United States. The rights accorded to a single individual are the same rights accorded to every citizen within the entire nation. In our cable license case, my and my Black American partners' loss of rights was attached to all Black Americans throughout the United States. The ability of governments to mistreat Black Americans was confirmed by a Black federal judge in Los Angeles who was appointed by a Democratic president. Doesn't fit the Democratic Party image, does it?

The same method of stealing the civil rights of those in South Central was applicable to the entire nation of minority urban communities. The commonality among all these communities was the Democratic Party and its willingness to forgo the constitutional rights of the citizens of these communities in order to develop favor with major contributors and large media companies.

In order to provide protected and unregulated monopolies to their friends, Democrats were willing to forgo justice and the rule of law under the Constitution for their citizens. Civil rights did not seem so important when they interfered with large Democratic contributors. This did not seem to affect the great liberal and progressive Democratic Party, but it proved they were neither liberal nor progressive.

They provide little more in the Black community than Black faces, which they pretended were representing the community but in fact represented the Democratic Party and its own pursuits—and these pursuits did not benefit urban minority communities. To the contrary, the Democratic Party and numerous Black politicians engaged in the passage of draconian laws penalizing urban Black communities for decades to come. Children would be locked up, often for life, at the age of sixteen or seventeen.

Black elected officials have shown themselves to be both ineffective and without the basic moral fiber we would expect from the leadership of a people who struggled for so long. Black elected officials and those who claim to be Black leaders have failed us. The failure is demonstrated in the lives of citizens of urban minority communities.

We must face the fact that the Democratic Party and Black elected officials have dramatically failed to improve the lives of Black Americans despite the rhetoric of the last forty-five years. It is necessary at this point to get rid of the leadership who put us in such a precarious position. That is certainly not to say that merely getting rid of the existing crop of failures will resolve all the problems in Black America. To once again quote James Baldwin, "Not everything that is faced can be changed, but nothing can be changed until it is faced." That is where we are in Black America today. We cannot afford to listen to the same rhetoric that has betrayed us both economically and as citizens, despite leadership's claims of integrity.

The public interest hypocrisy demonstrated by the Democratic Party in regard to issues affecting the entire nation is clearly visible. They do not seek relief from the issues closing in on South Central; rather, they seek to control these issues, under their own banner, for their own benefit. How can anyone take the word of a person who seeks to provide a solution to a problem that they willfully caused, as is the case in the broadband/cable television license debacle? This continuation of worthless leadership affects the entire United

188

States, has become an issue worthy of mass media coverage, and should spark numerous debates in the US Congress.

Why did they create the problem in the first place? Only an absence of integrity and civic-mindedness seems to provide the answer.

The issue of juvenile PTSD is one that can no longer be ignored. The causes of PTSD in urban and minority communities are the same as those experienced by soldiers on the battlefield. These conditions exist throughout South Central Los Angeles and numerous other urban minority communities in the United States. The refusal of government to address the issue of juvenile PTSD, which leads to gang involvement and criminal behavior, is an important factor in high rates of incarceration.

It is clear from the lack of information provided by the elected officials that helping the community face this issue is not a priority. The failure to address this severe problem within minority communities is a sign of the disconnect between political officials and the citizens they are supposed to be representing. This disconnect serves to deprive the communities of the ability to address this and many issues that affect them in a profound and negative way.

The inability to invest in your community is a contributing factor to the rise of gangs. The capital investment that is necessary to create jobs has been limited by the politics of betrayal. The gangs are part of the economic order within low-income and minority communities, and that issue must be addressed in order to find solutions to the gang problem.

The continuing calls for diversity within the entertainment industry cannot be effectively completed without an increase in Black ownership of media and its production. True diversity can only be accomplished through diversity of ownership so owners can determine what information is best suited to the market they are seeking to serve. The needs of urban minority communities are dramatically different than those of middle-income and upper-income families in other parts of any urban area. Black control and ownership in media, in my view, has been continually thwarted by representatives of the Democratic Party.

There is also the issue of abject nepotism in the Democratic Party in both New York and California. The city and state of New York have been controlled by the Cuomo family for more than thirty years. In California, the Brown family controlled the governor's office for thirty of the last sixty years. This does not give the appearance of democracy but rather of royalty passed down to family members disguised as a democracy. Family control of such enterprises has some similarity to family control of criminal enterprises.

Those with money are the ones who control the outcome of events within the society. It wasn't supposed to be that way, according to our Constitution. Those who are impacted are those without money, unable to change or adjust their fate. It is clear that Black America does not have a substantial degree of control over the events that affect them. The lack of understanding of the basic economic system under which we live puts many at a dramatic disadvantage.

How do we now address the issues caused by forty years of mistreatment and constitutional violations? The ability to counter these issues will take several generations at least, as I see it. However, with the dramatic change brought about by digital information sources, my estimates could be far off—change could be seen as soon as one generation or ten years. Having seen the many and varied changes that have occurred during the technology era, I hope that such change can occur within the Black community at the same general rate. They've been indoctrinated to this way of thinking by whatever means have been used, intentional or unintentional. It is not realistic to expect that these circumstances can be reversed over a short period of time when they have been ingrained into these children over many decades and generations.

I would be remiss if I did not provide a few potential solutions that I believe could be effective in altering the behavior of elected officials and the resulting government mistreatment of the disenfranchised. Let me start by saying that I believe the current two-party system has failed and is continuing to fail Black America and many other portions of America.

As a race of people, we must carefully examine our family structure. We have the largest percentage of single-parent families of any group in the US. I believe that a significant cause of this trend is the inability to establish the moral values of our own communities because we did not have access to or control of media. Another significant factor is the long-term prison sentences meted out to Black men, leaving many young men without access to positive male role models. Control of media is a determining factor in being able to establish morals and values among our children. Almost three out of four families in Black America are single-parent families. Statistics have clearly shown the disadvantages of children being raised by single parents instead of the traditional family unit. You will notice that the two-parent family has declined in Black America since we first sought to provide media and technology to the community in 1980.

The time has come for a third party to operate in the United States. We are the last industrialized democracy to maintain a two-party system. Many of our counterparts have third and fourth parties that serve to balance the two-party system with additional points of view and meaningful alternatives to the current policies instituted by the two-party system. The two-party system is failing right in front of our eyes.

A 2018 Gallup survey found that 57 percent of Americans said there needed to be a third major political party in the United States. Only 38 percent of Americans believed the two-party system was doing an acceptable job representing the American people. Third parties have significantly affected presidential races several times in recent history, such as with Ross Perot in 1992 and Ralph Nader in 2000. More than half of Democrats and one-third of Republicans support the call for a third party.

The third party would not be in control of government but would rather act as a fulcrum in order to balance the extremes that are shown by the current parties. I do not believe that Americans on either the Right or the Left are as extreme as the parties make them out to be. The use of a fulcrum could serve to balance the extremes that exist within our government today.

The development of a third party must start on a local basis in order to be effective. Let us moderate the behavior of our local governments and consider such moderation on a national basis. The small influence of a third party could have a dramatic effect upon the extremism and partisanship that is currently shown by the two parties within the United States.

Black America must dramatically increase its economic presence in the overall economy of the United States. The most important factor determining this involvement will be the utilization of capital income that is currently possessed by Black America. The mere spending of money is not a solution for an economy that has failed to serve Black America. We must make investments and become part of the economic fabric of this nation in order to become full citizens of the nation. This does not mean that every person must modify their behavior from consumer to investor. Rather, it means that those who possess the resources and desire must utilize such resources in order to stimulate our participation within the overall economy. Such participation in the overall economy will serve to help protect the rights that we seek. It has become clear that we cannot rely on political parties to ensure our rights within this nation.

We must create term limits for elected federal legislative officials just as we have created term limits for the presidency of the United States. We cannot allow elected officials to remain in office for thirty or forty years as society rapidly changes and they do not. The youth of America must be served, and they can only be served when there are openings in the government for them to participate within.

The concept of streaming is a new and dramatically changing method of delivering information without the requirement of massive quantities of capital, as was the case with cable or television. Digital media is the future. We must take advantage of the new opportunities that present themselves as society changes. Our best chance to participate in any of these changes is to limit our involvement with government officials.

Education is not merely that which is carried out in the classroom. People are in constant need of information and education in order to participate effectively in our society. The free press must be developed using new available technologies. The job of the free press is not merely to provide news but also information and education for those that have been failed by the education system.

In parting, may I say thank you to all those that I've encountered in my many travels across the United States. I have met so many more good people than bad people of every race, creed, and color that I am thankful to be living here in America despite the issues that we must face. I have the greatest belief that there are many people who seek to provide equal education and opportunity for all those within America, because that is the American way. Peace of the Lord be with you.

ABOUT THE AUTHOR

 Clinton E. Galloway is a Certified Public Accountant with a practice in Marina del Rey, California. He is also a registered securities principal and runs a registered securities broker-dealer, which is licensed by the Securities and Exchange Commission.

He was born in Birmingham, Alabama, but moved shortly thereafter with his family to New York City. He attended Northern Arizona University with the assistance of a baseball scholarship. In the late 1970s, after getting his CPA license, he relocated from a large international accounting firm in San Francisco to a major international investment banking firm in Beverly Hills.

His first book is titled *Anatomy of a Hustle: Cable Comes to South Central Los Angeles* (2012). This is his second book.

CPSIA information can be obtained
at www.ICGtesting.com
Printed in the USA
FSHW010030171220
76783FS